CONTEMPORARY DRUG POLICY

This book focuses on the use of drugs in our lives and how we respond to them. Whereas drug policy typically centers on the problems of illicit drugs or licit drugs used in illicit ways or circumstances, *Contemporary Drug Policy* instead considers the wide variety of substances we call drugs as a normal part of our personal and social experience and asks how and when drugs benefit us as well as how and when they are harmful.

The evidence is clear that at some times, in some circumstances, and in some places drugs are a problem. This book does not ignore these issues but shifts our attention to making policies that also recognize their legitimate and constructive place in society. It focuses on asking questions, challenging assumptions, and developing responses to drugs based on evidence from scientific study as directed by critical criminological theory rather than mainstream theory or unfounded assumptions.

Different from other books on drug policy, this book does not offer answers or solutions. Rather it shows how critical criminological theories can lead scientific research in new directions supportive of policies that offer both solutions to problems that are found to be related to drugs and an appreciation for the benefits that drugs can bring to people and society. This book will be of interest to those studying or researching drug policy as well as professionals involved in policy-making processes.

Henry H. Brownstein is a Senior Fellow in the Substance Abuse, Mental Health and Criminal Justice Studies Department at NORC at the University of Chicago, USA. For almost 30 years he has been studying drug policy, drugs and crime, and drug markets. He has published several books and dozens of articles and book chapters on topics including drug policy, drugs and violence, drug markets, qualitative research methods, and the relationship between research and policy. He earned his PhD in sociology in 1977 from Temple University, USA.

New Directions in Critical Criminology
Edited by Walter S. DeKeseredy
UNIVERSITY OF ONTARIO INSTITUTE OF TECHNOLOGY

This series presents new cutting-edge critical criminological empirical, theoretical, and policy work on a broad range of social problems, including drug policy, rural crime and social control, policing and the media, ecocide, intersectionality, and the gendered nature of crime. It aims to highlight the most up-to-date authoritative essays written by new and established scholars in the field. Rather than offering a survey of the literature, each book takes a strong position on topics of major concern to those interested in seeking new ways of thinking critically about crime.

1. Contemporary Drug Policy
Henry H. Brownstein

//
CONTEMPORARY DRUG POLICY

Henry H. Brownstein

Routledge
Taylor & Francis Group
LONDON AND NEW YORK

To my daughters and their husbands
as they start their lives together
Becky and Mike Howard
Liz and Alex Gyde

First published 2013
by Routledge
2 Park Square, Milton Park, Abingdon, Oxon, OX14 4RN

Simultaneously published in the USA and Canada
by Routledge
711 Third Avenue, New York, NY 10017

Routledge is an imprint of the Taylor & Francis Group, an informa business

© 2013 Henry H. Brownstein

The right of Henry H. Brownstein to be identified as the author of this work has been asserted by him in accordance with sections 77 and 78 of the Copyright, Designs and Patents Act 1988.

All rights reserved. No part of this book may be reprinted or reproduced or utilized in any form or by any electronic, mechanical, or other means, now known or hereafter invented, including photocopying and recording, or in any information storage or retrieval system, without permission in writing from the publishers.

British Library Cataloguing in Publication Data
A catalogue record for this book is available from the British Library

Library of Congress Cataloging in Publication Data
A catalog record has been requested for this book

ISBN: 978-0-415-63536-3 (hbk)
ISBN: 978-0-415-63537-0 (pbk)
ISBN: 978-0-203-09345-0 (ebk)

Typeset in Bembo
by Taylor & Francis Books

Printed and bound in Great Britain by the MPG Books Group

CONTENTS

Preface and acknowledgments   *vi*

1 Informing and guiding drug policy   1

2 The debate over control and regulation   20

3 The debate over management   37

4 The debate over value   52

5 Case studies: the unintended consequences of ill-informed policies   71

6 False issues, dubious solutions, and the need for public discourse   86

References   *98*
Index   *113*

PREFACE AND ACKNOWLEDGMENTS

Preface

My interest in drugs and drug policy goes back to the 1980s when I was working as a researcher for the New York State Division of Criminal Justice Services (DCJS). Our office at DCJS was established by the Governor to collect and maintain data on crime and justice, to use those data to produce statistics and do analyses that would result in reports that would inform relevant state policymakers, and to analyze and recommend policy proposals that would help the government to deal with the problems faced by the state. During that time the state was confronted by the introduction of crack cocaine in New York City with its rapidly expanding markets and apparent harm to users and the people around them. Almost immediately crack cocaine as a problem overwhelmed policymakers and practitioners, drawing enormous attention and resources. And it came on the scene so quickly that no one really knew what was happening or what to do about it.

As the researcher in the office most interested in studying and understanding what was happening with crack and what might be done, I was introduced to Paul Goldstein, a researcher at an organization in New York City, Narcotic and Drug Research, Inc. (NDRI). Government policymakers were particularly concerned about what appeared to be a relationship between crack and violence, and Paul had been writing and talking about ways that drugs and violence in general might possibly be related. He and I started working together and, over the years, with support from the National Institute of Justice and the National Institute on Drug Abuse did a series of studies on the involvement of drugs in crime and violence. Our first studies together were specifically on crack and homicide, but our work subseqently expanded and our findings resulted in lots of new questions about the relationship between drugs and crime and violence and about how the government, the media, policymakers, and practitioners were responding to a problem they did not really understand or even know very much about.

After leaving the government and teaching at a university and continuing my research for a number of years, in 2000 I accepted a position as Director of the Drugs and Crime Research Division at the National Institute of Justice (NIJ). My job was to oversee the awarding of grants to researchers studying drugs and crime, to establish a national agenda to guide that research, and to provide leadership to an NIJ program that was collecting interview data and urine samples from arrestees within 48 hours of arrest in 35 counties around the country—Arrestee Drug Abuse Monitoring (ADAM). I was only there for four years, but during that time I got to meet and know many of the social scientists in the US and other nations doing research in this area, including people doing research who asked questions about public health as well as public safety. I also got to meet many of the people advocating one drug policy position or another. And again I ended up with more questions than answers about why we were doing what we were doing in response to what was considered to be a problem associated with drugs in society.

More recently my work in the area of drugs and crime and violence shifted specifically to drug markets. In 2011 at NORC at the University of Chicago I completed a study funded by the National Institute on Drug Abuse of the dynamics of methamphetamine markets in America. My colleagues and I started out thinking we knew something about drug markets and, after four years of travelling around the country talking to people who lived their lives in the belly and in the shadows of methamphetamine markets, I realized something I should have known when I started: meth is not crack and meth markets are not like crack markets. So once again I came away with more questions than answers.

The purpose of this book is to discuss drug policy in a way that raises more questions than answers. The book takes a critical look at drug policy from a philosophical and theoretical perspective. It illustrates and explains how established policies and practices designed to address real and imagined problems of and associated with drug use, involvement, and distribution are grounded in theories and beliefs that are not always supported by solid evidence and are often in fact built on a foundation of unfounded assumptions or theories that lead in directions that are not always productive.

What we call drugs are really not one but a lot of different things, and people use different drugs for lots of different reasons, some of which are good and others not, and lots of people just like using drugs. Alcohol and caffeine, for example, are extremely popular among large segments of many populations just for how they make the user feel or how they make them feel among other people. Other drugs, like marijuana, are very popular among more limited but large segments of populations, both for recreational and therapeutic purposes. Other drugs, some of which make the user high and others which make the user low, have smaller but nonetheless committed followings, like cocaine, heroin, and methamphetamine. Certain other drugs, such as aspirin or acetaminophen, are widely available and commonly used because some government authority has declared them safe and healing. Others are used selectively for more serious healing because while they have scientifically established therapeutic value they are only legally available when sanctioned by a certified medical provider; of course there are people who find ways to get these drugs even if not officially sanctioned for their personal use because they are curious or like what the drug does for them. So particular drugs can serve a social good and they can be good for people, but it is also fair to say that particular drugs that are used in inappropriate ways or at an inappropriate time or sometimes even just used at all can be a source of harm to individuals or to others around them.

This book is about the substances we call drugs, how they fit into our lives, and how we respond to them. But whereas drug policy typically focuses on drugs as a singular phenomenon and on the problems of illicit drugs or licit drugs used in illicit ways or circumstances, in this book we instead consider the wide variety of substances we call drugs as a normal part of our personal and social experience and ask how and when different drugs can or do benefit us as well as how and when they can be or are harmful. The evidence is clear that at some times, in some circumstances, and in some places some drugs are a problem for some people. This book does not ignore the problems associated with all or any of the substances we call drugs, but shifts attention to making policies that also recognize that they have a legitimate and constructive place in society. Instead of pretending to have answers, the book focuses on asking questions, questioning assumptions, and seeking to find responses to the good and bad consequences of the various substances we call drugs based on evidence from scientific study as directed by critical criminological theory rather than mainstream theory or unfounded assumptions. It shows how research grounded in critical criminological theory can lead science and thus policy toward more reasonable, responsible, and just drug policy.

Rather than argue for a particular policy position, this book argues simply that there is a need for more open and honest discourse that considers the broader place in society of all the substances we call drugs. It considers different drug policy perspectives asking questions about how the perspective is informed (or not) by scientific evidence and how ideology and theory offer direction for the scientific research that has been done or needs to be done to identify and address the right questions. Chapters 2 through 4 each focuses on a particular area for discourse or debate about drug policy. Each gives special attention to how mainstream criminological theories have moved science toward research that has supported the making of policy in a particular direction that has not been particularly effective in finding the appropriate and most productive (i.e. more beneficial than harmful) place for drugs in society. Then each considers how research grounded in critical criminological theory could lead science and thus policy in a different and more productive direction. Chapter 5 gives two examples to illustrate the challenge of making drug policy. The first and last chapters offer an introduction and a conclusion to making the case that creating drug policy is a challenge and why and how an open and honest discourse or debate at this time would be so valuable.

Acknowledgments and disclaimer

At a recent meeting of the American Society of Criminology I ran into Walter DeKeseredy. Walter was sitting with Tom Sutton and after introducing us I sat down with them for a while. As old friends do when they meet at professional conferences, we talked about our latest professional work and caught up on personal stuff. Then Walter mentioned that he was working with Tom, a Commissioning Editor in Criminology for Routledge, and was editing a series of books on new directions in critical criminology. For about 30 years, and all the time I have known Walter, I have been doing research or working on government projects related to drugs and crime or drug policy, so they asked me if I would consider writing a book for the series examining drugs and public policy from a critical perspective. Several emails, a prospectus submitted, and favorable comments from anonymous reviewers later I started to write. This was an opportunity to write something and make an argument I have wanted to make for a long time, so I gratefully thank Walter and Tom for making it possible. I also thank Nicola Hartley at Routledge for helping me to turn my manuscript into a book and the anonymous reviewers for their helpful comments and recommendations.

As I was writing I got deep into the text and worried I was getting lost in the details of the narrative and losing sight of the main arguments I was trying to make and what I was trying to say. So I asked Marty Schwartz to read the first chapter to see if he thought perhaps I was drifting too far. Without hesitation, Marty read the chapter and gave me his comments and recommendations. So I thank him for helping me keep my writing focused and the manuscript moving forward.

The research I write about in Chapter 5 was done over several decades with a number of colleagues, most notably at various times with Paul Goldstein, Barry Spunt, Susan Crimmins, Bruce Taylor, Tim Mulcahy, and Johannes Fernandes-Huessy. The research was largely funded by grants from the National Institute on Drug Abuse (NIDA) of the US Department of Health and Human Services and the National Institute of Justice (NIJ) of the US Department of Justice. I wrote this book while an employee of NORC at the University of Chicago and I thank my friends and colleagues at NORC for their encouragement. Mostly I thank Eric Gopelrud and Dan Gaylin for their support and Dave Kaplan, Curt Bailey, and Jim Dunne for their advice.

While I thank everyone for their help in getting this book written, I take full responsibility for what I wrote. Opinions and points of view herein are mine alone and do not represent those of any other individual or organization, including NORC, NIDA, or NIJ.

1
INFORMING AND GUIDING DRUG POLICY

Throughout history the use of pharmacological substances to preserve or sustain personal health and well-being has had a lawful and reputable place in most every society. At the same time science and experience have shown us that consuming certain drugs can be harmful to the people who use them or to others around them, as can misuse of any drug. But we also know from science and experience that drugs can do good things for us. Today healthcare professionals routinely recommend and provide assorted drugs to deal not only with the serious physical and mental ailments that individuals present to them, but also with the ordinary pains and stresses of everyday life. So it should not be surprising that with or without the recommendation of a healthcare provider so many people seek and find drugs to make them feel better, or at least different. Aldous Huxley once wrote, "That humanity at large will ever be able to dispense with Artificial Paradises seems very unlikely. Most men and women lead lives at worst so painful, at the best so monotonous, poor and limited that the urge to escape, the longing to transcend themselves if only for a few moments, is and has always been one of the principal appetites of the soul" (Huxley 1954: 62).

Huxley's view of human experience may have been a bit dismal, but his point is not without merit. There are positive things that drugs do for people and those things have been widely recognized and legitimated. The therapeutic value and uses for any number of drugs are well documented. So even if there are drugs that are known to cause problems or problems known to be caused by the way or ways in which drugs are used or misused, it would be hard to imagine that the use of drugs can ever or anywhere be banished. As Andrew Weil wrote, "Like the fantasy that drugs can be made to go away, the idea that people who want drugs can be discouraged from using them is an impossible dream that gets us nowhere except in worse trouble" (Weil 1972: 189).

This book is about contemporary drug policy. It considers how we got where we are regarding the use and misuse of pharmacological substances that have the capacity to influence how we feel and how we act. It considers the way and ways we have responded to the problems we face or believe we face in relation to the use and misuse of these substances, and in doing so how we have applied our knowledge or lack of knowledge about how drugs in general or in particular can be beneficial or harmful to people or their communities. It places these considerations in the context of history, culture, ideology, and science to explain how not only knowledge but also beliefs and values are and have been used to justify our decisions and actions regarding drugs and what to do or not do with and about them. The book does this by looking at the different debates or discourses that underlie much of what has come to pass as drug policy.

The problem of morphine

Consider morphine. Morphine is an opioid medication used to treat moderate or even severe pain. During a keynote address to the annual meeting of the American Society of Regional Anesthesia in 1995, Laurence Mather noted that morphine in one form or another "is the oldest pain-relieving agent still in therapeutic use" having been around for "at least several millennia" (Mather 1995: 263, 262). Ongoing research has identified potential health concerns or risks associated with morphine use in some circumstances and some limitations in its capacity to relieve pain (e.g. Chou *et al.* 2009; Chu *et al.* 2006; Kestin 1993; Reisman 2011). Nonetheless, throughout the world its value as a pain reliever continues to be widely recognized (Kalso and Vainio 1990; Pergolizzi *et al.* 2008;

Pizzo and Clark 2012; World Health Organization 2007, 2000). Mather concluded his lecture by exclaiming that "morphine still makes as good pharmacologic and clinical sense as ever!" (Mather 1995: 279).

Despite having a recognized pharmacologic value as a pain reliever, morphine is not equally available in all parts of the world to all people who could benefit from its use. During his address to representatives from 192 member nations at the 58th session of the World Health Assembly in Vienna in 2005, Hamid Ghodse, then President of the International Narcotics Control Board (INCB), raised concern about the availability throughout the world of narcotic drugs essential for medicine and science (United Nations Information Service 2005). In particular, he expressed concern about the lack of opioid analgesics available to people suffering from cancer and AIDS in developing nations. He referred to the 2003 INCB Annual Report that found "the share of developing countries in the global consumption of morphine continues to be only about 6 per cent, although those countries account for almost 80 percent of the world population" (International Narcotics Control Board 2003: 29).

More recently concern for inadequate access to needed analgesics in developing nations, in particular opioids, was expressed in a report issued by the World Health Organization (WHO). According to the WHO report:

> In spite of adequate supply of opioids raw materials worldwide, in many parts of the world, patients suffering severe pain as a result of diseases such as cancer face immense challenges in obtaining pain relief. In many countries opioid medicines that could provide effective relief are not available in sufficient quantities. In other words, severe pain is often left untreated, although eliminating it is clinically possible. Unrelieved severe and prolonged pain causes immense suffering and has devastating effects on individuals, their families and the communities to which they belong.
>
> *(WHO 2007: 5)*

The WHO publication not only described the significance of the problem in developing nations, but also suggested possible explanations (WHO 2007: 7–8): (1) While certain substances do need to be regulated, when regulations are applied in a manner that is "inappropriately restrictive" they become "impediments to access to adequate patient care." (2) Regulators, policymakers, medical personnel, and even patients and their family members have misconceptions about the appropriate use of opioids under contemporary medical standards of care, and their lack of knowledge and ill-informed attitudes become an impediment to adequate and appropriate use. (3) Independent of the impediments due to restrictive regulation, inadequate knowledge, and ill-informed attitudes, another impediment in developing nations is the lack of resources needed to procure the drugs and an "insufficient medical infrastructure."

The point is that both historical and scientific evidence support the conclusion that morphine has exceptional palliative properties so that when it is properly and appropriately used it can reduce suffering for people experiencing not only moderate but even severe pain. Yet the record shows that despite this knowledge most of the people in the world who suffer the pain of cancer, AIDS, or the like do not have access to morphine.

Morphine is the main active compound in opium and is obtained from the juice secreted from the seed pods of the poppy plant (Kestin 1993). According to the 2011 Annual Report of the United Nations Office on Drugs and Crime, the first decade of the twenty-first century saw a decline in opium poppy cultivation before it rose in 2010, mainly due to increasing cultivation in Myanmar (UNODC 2011: 20). The same Report noted that opium is cultivated in a number of places around the globe besides Myanmar, including Mexico, Colombia, India, Thailand, and Laos (UNODC 2011: 59). But the bulk of cultivation and production takes place in Afghanistan: in 2010 almost two-thirds of the world's poppy supply was cultivated there (123,000 hectares) and almost three-fourths of the world's opium was produced there (4,860 metric tons, compared to 7,853 in 2009), though overall production worldwide including Afghanistan has declined in recent years (UNODC 2011: 45).

Arguably then the declining production of opioid pain medicines could help explain the shortage. But as the WHO report made clear, it is not that simple. The problem is not just about the adequacy of the supply but more so about its distribution. Thus the explanation is not simply an insufficient supply of poppy plants or declining opium production. There are political as well as economic considerations. The illicit use of opium particularly in the form of heroin is considered a health and safety crisis in parts of the world, particularly the West. Nonetheless, in 2009 there was an estimated $68 billion in revenue earned by illicit traffickers. Since it was illegal, in Afghanistan that trade largely benefited anti-government elements and did little for the legitimate Afghan economy (UNODC 2011: 83).

An argument could be made that it might be beneficial to the health and well-being of people in developing nations who are suffering from serious pain and to the economies of developing nations like Afghanistan if we could reconsider some form of legitimate cultivation and production of opium in Afghanistan and other producing nations (Anderson 2010; Aslan 2008; Attaran and Boozary 2011; Chouvy 2008; Rubin 2000). That is not to say that opium production would or should suddenly become a legitimate industry in Afghanistan, only that it might be good for people on different sides of the issue to talk about it. But things like that do not happen easily. And that is the underlying problem of drug policy in the contemporary world. Our actions and decisions in response to the use and misuse of licit and illicit substances for personal consumption may be expressed in the language of the public good, but inevitably they are ensnared by the forces of economics and politics. And in this world of drug policy some of us are guided by science through knowledge and reason and others by ideology through beliefs and values, making an open and productive dialogue at best difficult.

Drug policy in recent centuries

Drugs were not always and not everywhere considered a cause of crime and violence or an explanation for problems of health and well-being. There has been considerable variation over time and across national boundaries. As the example of morphine suggests, to some extent that variation is related to the relationships between more powerful and developed nations and less powerful and developed nations. The examples below suggest that the variation is also related to relationships between more and less powerful people and interest groups within nations.

In the US from the founding of the nation to the end of the nineteenth century pharmacological substances in the form of home remedies were widely available to anyone who needed relief from illness or pain or any other ailment, with unspecified ingredients often including opium or cocaine (Inciardi 2007; Musto 1991). A person could purchase a hypodermic kit for using morphine from the Sears Roebuck catalog and a new soft drink, Coca-Cola, actually included extracts of coca to give consumers an extra lift. The Bayer Company introduced a new product named Heroin for coughs and other chest ailments. David Musto described the late nineteenth century in America as "an era of wide availability and unrestrained advertising" (Musto 1991: 42). Interestingly, the limited control in the US in part was due to the fact that each state had its own authority to regulate medical practice and pharmacological products, so there was no central policy. The situation was not necessarily restrictive but was more coordinated in nations with centralized national authority, such as Britain.

During that time concerns for health and safety were not the driving force behind drug policy. Only later was there the conviction that drugs were a danger to people and their communities and that consequently policies and programs were needed to protect the health and safety of those people and communities. But even then there was not consensus about what the problem was and how to deal with it. The medical community focused on things like addiction and declared drugs a health problem and the criminal justice community focused on people taking advantage of the demand for drugs by others in dishonest ways and declared drugs a crime problem (Inciardi 2007; Musto 1999, 1991). That lack of consensus continues in one form or another to the present, but the theme that underlies drug policy in either case involves the demonization of certain drugs and the people who use them.

By the early twentieth century in the US efforts to take charge of what had popularly come to be seen as a national drug epidemic were underway, with the federal government looking for ways to gain control over what had all along been a responsibility of the states. The Pure Food and Drug Act was passed in 1906 and while it did not help the federal government gain control of the sale of what were considered addictive or problematic drugs, it did set standards for quality, packaging, and labeling of patent medicines sold through interstate commerce (Musto 1991: 43). The federal government did eventually establish its authority in dealing with drugs when it passed the Harrison Act in 1914 and the Marijuana Tax Act in 1937, both tax acts that offered some federal power through taxation in the areas of regulation and control regarding production, importation, sale, purchase, and distribution of drugs classified as narcotics and marijuana (Kaplan 1971; Musto 1999; Smith 1988).

Interest in marijuana in particular was sparked in the US during the 1930s when the depressed economy was accompanied by increases in crime, violence, and marijuana use. In 1930 the Federal Bureau of Narcotics (FBN) was formed and Harry Anslinger became its Commissioner. Anslinger served in that role from 1930 to 1962 and during that time advanced policies that were tough on drug users, especially marijuana users, and used his position as a platform to invigorate the demonization of drugs and drug users (Inciardi 2007; Kaplan 1971; McWilliams 1990). The theme of these efforts was prohibition.

In 1969 President Richard Nixon addressed the US Congress to inform its members that drug abuse should be considered a serious national threat, and in 1971 he formally declared war on drugs (Inciardi 2007; Weisheit 1990; Wisotsky 1986). The declaration of war effectively shifted attention from drug users to drug trafficking and in 1973 Nixon created the Drug Enforcement Administration (DEA) within the US Department of Justice to fight the war against drug trafficking. But the war did not truly begin until Ronald Reagan became President and reaffirmed the declaration. Then his successor, George H.W. Bush, with Congress passed the Anti-Drug Abuse Act of 1988 and formed the Office of National Drug Control Policy (ONDCP). Bush appointed William Bennett as his first ONDCP Director, also called the "drug czar," and the war was underway. In the US the war on drugs focused on trafficking rather than use, with most of the attention from the start going to the supply of drugs rather than the demand for drugs, with funding for combined law enforcement, incarceration, and interdiction activities regularly exceeding combined funding for prevention and treatment (ONDCP 2012a, 1989).

Not every nation followed the same policy direction as the US. Many focused more on the reduction of harm related to drugs rather than to the prohibition of illicit drug use and control over drug users and traffickers. For example, in the Netherlands the focus of drug policy has been on health protection and the reduction of health risk with special interest in the prevention of drug use and the treatment and rehabilitation of users, the reduction of harm to users, diminishing any public nuisance related to drug users, and then combating production and trafficking (van Laar *et al.* 2011). Similarly in the UK the emphasis has been on harm reduction going back to 1926 with the release of *The Report of the Departmental Committee on Morphine and Heroin* (Bennett 1988).

On the international level, cooperation on drug policy commenced in 1909 at a gathering of 13 nations meeting in Shanghai for the International Opium Commission (Musto 1991: 43). The focus was on opium and opiates and while resolutions were adopted no binding decisions were made and no treaties signed. This was followed by an international conference of 12 nations in the Hague in 1911 that resulted in the nations present agreeing to enact domestic legislation to control trade in narcotics and to fund education campaigns. More recently on the international level the legal and administrative framework for international agreements on drug policy is based on three Conventions negotiated among nations under the auspices of the United Nations (Bewley-Taylor 2003; Sinha 2001; UN 1988, 1971, 1961). The Single Convention in 1961 consolidated all former multinational treaties negotiated from 1912 to 1953 and tightened controls over 100 different substances considered narcotic drugs (UN 1961). The Convention on Psychotropic Substances extended international control to synthetic psychotropic substances (UN 1971), and the Convention against Illicit Traffic in Narcotic Drugs and Psychotropic Substances in 1988 sought to complement the other two by focusing on international drug trafficking (UN 1988). Overall, the three drug Conventions focused on the supply of drugs rather than demand for drugs and were oriented to prohibition and criminalization rather than treatment, thereby limiting the flexibility of independent nations to develop their own drug policies (Bewley-Taylor 2003; Room and Reuter 2011). In a report to the Canadian Parliament, Jay Sinha suggested that this situation is the consequence of values and the relationships between more and less powerful nations. He wrote, "Beginning in an era of morally tainted racism and colonial trade wars, prohibition-based drug control grew to international proportions at the insistence of the United States" (Sinha 2001: 37). As a result arguments have been made that "the system has had very little overall success in controlling the supply of drugs" (Sinha 2001: 37) and that "increasing numbers of states are reviewing their stance on the international treaties" (Bewley-Taylor 2003: 171).

Guiding drug policy: science and theory, ideology and values

From science we can learn things about the biochemical, physiological, psychological, economic, and sociological explanations for using drugs or being involved with illicit drugs, and the consequences of use or involvement for people, their families, and their communities. At its best, science helps us distinguish with confidence what we know from what we do not know and directs us to subsequent studies to learn more about those things we cannot and should not feel certain we already know. The challenge is to find the direction to follow and to know when your findings and conclusions are defensible, trustworthy, logical, and reasonable so that they add to our accumulated body of knowledge, point us toward the next set of pertinent research questions, and ultimately are able to inform policy decisions and actions.

Ideally, theory guides the progression of scientific study by suggesting how we might explain what we do not know, thus helping us to get from one bit of established knowledge to another to advance our understanding and capacity to explain. As Herbert Blumer wrote, "The aim of theory in empirical science is to develop analytic schemes of the empirical world with which the given science is concerned [thereby] setting problems, staking out objects, and leading inquiry into asserted relations" (Blumer 1969: 140–41). In reality it is more complicated than that. Knowledge is never absolute so untested assumptions get used to fill the gaps, and those assumptions can make things tricky. As a cautionary note, some time ago Thomas Szasz told us that "ideas do have practical consequences, and although social policies usually rest on and are justified by ideas, the fact remains that ideas can be fully effective only against other ideas" (Szasz 1982: 762). As Szasz went on to explain it, arguments can be used to rebut other arguments but cannot directly cause change in a social policy. So we have to be careful how we think about ideas and how we use them.

We can easily be led astray when we use assumptions in the form of untested ideas to inform the gaps in our knowledge and point us toward our next questions, especially when the ideas are grounded in beliefs, values, or attitudes and become ideological. Based on an extensive review of writings on the concept of ideology, Hamilton proposed the following definition: "An ideology is a system of collectively held normative and reputedly factual ideas and beliefs and attitudes advocating a particular pattern of social relationships and arrangements, and/or aimed at justifying a particular pattern of conduct, which its proponents seek to promote, realise, pursue or maintain" (Hamilton 1987: 38). The problem then of using ideology as a guide in our search for useful knowledge is that facts are only reputed and observations or findings are used to advocate for and justify something being endorsed (cf. Gauchat 2012; Leiss 1975).

Ideology can make it tempting to accept unverifiable assumptions and to follow those wherever they lead. The National Institutes of Health (NIH) comprise the leading federal agency in the US supporting medical and scientific research aimed at improving the health of the nation. In 2003 the NIH was forced to justify "about 200 approved or funded projects to the House Committee on Energy and Commerce after being questioned about controversial research topics such as sexual behavior" (Kaiser 2003: 758). Specifically, the grants were being questioned by a conservative advocacy group concerned that the NIH was funding studies involving things like sexuality, HIV/AIDS transmission, and drug use. Alan Leshner, chief executive officer of the American Association for the Advancement of Science and former director of the National Institute on Drug Abuse (NIDA), an institute of the NIH, responded in an editorial published in *Science*. The editorial was called "Don't let ideology trump science" and he wrote, "Whenever science is attacked on ideological grounds, its integrity and usefulness are threatened. Society cannot afford for moralistic dogma to replace scientific judgment when the public's welfare is at stake" (Leshner 2003: 1479).

In summary, guided by unsubstantiated beliefs, values, and attitudes, ideology moves the production of knowledge in a preferred direction that can be used to justify advocacy for a favored position or policy. Theory, on the other hand, is a part of the scientific enterprise the purpose of which is to help us to understand and explain reality by generating propositions that become hypotheses to be tested and confirmed, or not, by established scientific methods, repeatedly resulting in new propositions for further testing and confirmation as new knowledge accumulates (cf. Chafetz 1978; Kuhn 1977; Popper 1959). Naturally this is an ideal and is not always realized. So Kuhn proposed five characteristics that must be present for a theory to be a good scientific theory: accuracy, consistency, scope, simplicity, and fruitfulness (Kuhn 1977: 321). That is, by definition while ideology is intended to influence knowledge construction in the direction of desired outcomes, theory ideally is intended to be an objective and unbiased guide for scientific inquiry that can lead toward informed, realistic, and constructive public policy.

Arguably, ideology has been a major driver of contemporary drug policy. Reflecting the social and cultural tensions of the twentieth century, in the shadows of the war on drugs has lurked a moralistic ideology about the weakness of drug users and the evil of drug dealers (Bakalar and Grinspoon 1984). In the US, for example, the emphasis of the drug war has been on control and prohibition and has been nourished by the powerful tensions separating people by socio-economic category, ethnic and minority status, generational order, and gender (Musto 1999). Sociologist Troy Duster studied the evolution of drug policy in the US in the 1900s in terms of the social, legal, and moral activity around drug use and observed that whereas most people addicted to drugs in 1969 were black males from lower and working class homes, in 1900 most were middle class and middle-aged white females (Duster 1970: 20–21). Based on his observations and findings he concluded, "middle America's moral hostility comes faster and easier when directed toward a young, lower-class Negro male, than toward a middle-aged white female" (Duster 1970: 21). Others who studied drug policy in the US have come to similar conclusions about how it evolved over time. Marijuana became a villain in the 1920s and 1930s when its visible users were disproportionately black men in the South and Mexicans in the Southwest (Inciardi 2007; Sloman 1979). During the 1960s and 1970s when cocaine in powder form was expensive and use was limited to middle and upper class mostly white users it was accepted if not approved (Inciardi 2007), but in the 1980s when it was sold in inexpensive rocks as crack to poor, minority users it became a demon drug (Williams 1992).

While ideology has had and continues to have an influence on drug policy, theory has had an influence as well through its role in guiding science toward the production of new knowledge that can inform policy. In this book we consider the role of theory as a force in the determination of contemporary drug policy. Since the focus of drug policy tends to be on the illicit rather than the licit side of drug use, misuse, and distribution, we emphasize criminological theory. Also, criminological theory gives us a broad explanatory framework for guiding scientific inquiry in that through its various paradigms and manifestations it integrates sociological, psychological, economic, as well as physiological and biochemical explanations of drug involvement (Akers and Sellers 2008; Bohm and Vogel 2011; Curran and Renzetti 2001).

Different from ideology, ideally theory is part of the scientific process of building knowledge (Kuhn 1977). But like ideology, theories are also dependent on assumptions. In his critique of contemporary social theory in the later middle of the twentieth century, Alvin Gouldner argued that every theory "has both political and personal relevance, which, according to the technical canons of social theory, it is not supposed to have" (Gouldner 1970: 41). He suggested that all theories include two types of assumptions: postulations are those that are explicitly formulated from what is learned and known and background assumptions are those that come to us through our personal experience of culture and socialization (Gouldner 1970: 29). Postulations therefore are part of the scientific process, but background assumptions are brought to the theory by the theorist from his or her everyday life experience, a reality that has been described as "taken for granted" in the sense that it is "simply there, as [a] self-evident and compelling facticity" (Berger and Luckmann 1966: 23). Reflecting on Gouldner's argument, Fuhrman wrote, "It was not that evidence, logic and coherence did not count but these only partially constituted social theory. In Gouldner's world the production of social theory also depended on dreams, imaginations and feelings of the theorist" (Fuhrman 1989: 358). That is, even theories are not totally value free.

In criminology there are well-defined differences between mainstream and critical criminological theories (Gibbs 1987; Taylor *et al.* 1973). In simple terms, mainstream criminological theory grew out of the classical, neo-classical, and positivist thought of earlier times and today in its various expressions proposes ideas that explain deviant and criminal behavior in the context of things like social disorganization, social control and bonding, socialization and differential association, and anomie and strain supporting social policies that view society as essentially sound in need perhaps of reform but certainly not transformation (Akers and Sellers 2008; Curran and Renzetti 2001; Jacoby 2004; Lilly *et al.* 2011). Similarly, critical criminological theory grew from the Marxist paradigm and today in its various expressions proposes ideas that explain how notions of crime and deviance are constructed or how and why people come to be labeled as criminal or deviant in the context of the unequal distribution of power and material resources supporting social policies that redress or at least address those inequalities recognizing the fatal faults and flaws inherent in the structure of society (DeKeseredy 2011; DeKeseredy and Dragiweicz 2012; Schwartz and Hatty 2003).

For our purposes the important point here is that mainstream and critical criminological theories not only have different philosophical roots, but they are based on different assumptions and lead in different scientific and policy directions (Bohm and Vogel 2011; Einstadter and Henry 2006). In describing criminology as a science Edwin Sutherland suggested that criminological theory should develop "a body of general and verified principles and other types of knowledge regarding this process of law, crime, and reaction to crime" (Sutherland and Cressey 1974: 3). Then the theory could guide the scientist trying to understand and explain crime and justice, though there would always remain gaps that would have to be filled by "preliminary research findings and unverifiable assumptions" (Zahn *et al.* 2004: 16). Philosophical assumptions would have to be made about questions that had not yet been answered or might even be unanswerable about things like whether certain behavior is good or bad or right or wrong, what is the nature of reality, and even where does knowledge come from (Bohm and Vogel 2011: 4). Different criminological theories make different assumptions to answer these questions and thereby fill out their explanations so that they guide subsequent ideas and research in one direction or another.

For policy the issue is how different theories given different assumptions move policy in different directions. When Donald Cressey was given the Edwin H. Sutherland Award by the American Society of Criminology on November 4, 1967, he concluded that the way criminologists viewed crime and criminal behavior was about to undergo a major change in direction. He observed that among criminologists in the field there was a "growing awareness that criminality is not 'in' people and, therefore, does not 'come out' in form such that it can simply be observed and then recorded in statistics on murder, rape, or any other crime or delinquency" (Cressey 1968: 5). Therefore, he predicted that criminology would increasingly recognize the interrelatedness of the components of the process of doing justice and become more interdisciplinary, moving in the direction of what he called "negotiated justice" (Cressey 1968: 6). Writing about that observation and prediction years later, he confessed that he was wrong. He wrote, "In 1967, of course, no one knew that the Law Enforcement Assistance Administration was going to throw billions into a war on crime or that the so-called 'research arm' of LEAA, the National Institute of Law Enforcement and Administration of Justice, was going to be more interested in financing studies about what to do about 'the crime problem' than in financing studies about why there is a 'crime problem' to worry about" (Cressey 1978: 171). He concluded that the result was that criminologists abandoned the search for "valid propositions stated in a causal framework" (Cressey 1978: 173) and with their loss of attention to science became contributors to a "repressive war on crime" (Cressey 1978: 184).

Cressey went on to argue that with the attraction of getting funding for their research from the federal government through the LEAA, criminologists—who had been working as scientists doing research to search for new knowledge that might inform policy and policymakers—turned their attention to trying to directly influence those policies and policymakers. He suggested that the criminologist in the US in the later twentieth century had become "a technical assistant to politicians bent on repressing crime, rather than a scientist seeking valid propositions stated in a causal framework" (Cressey 1978: 173). He proposed that instead of becoming "policy advisors in this repressive war on crime" that criminologists should turn their attention to studying "conditions under which criminal laws are enacted, enforced, and broken" and then maybe they could "come up with some reasonable generalizations" and "politicians might listen to them, just as politicians listened to Bentham, Becccaria, Voltaire, and even Freud" (Cressey 1978: 184–85).

Given Cressey's conclusion, for drug policy, and for any policy, the prerequisite for good policy is to be able to base decisions and actions on knowledge in which the policymaker can have confidence. Accordingly, it is the responsibility of the scientist who wants to contribute to policy to work independent of the policy arena to do the research that will produce valid, reliable, and trustworthy knowledge that can be used to inform the policymaker. In his powerful analysis of the war on drugs in the US, near the end of the twentieth century Elliott Currie opens by saying, "The failure of American drug policy is depressingly apparent. Twenty years of the 'war' on drugs have jammed our jails and prisons, immobilized the criminal justice system in many cities, swollen the ranks of the criminalized and unemployable minority poor, and diverted desperately needed resources from other social needs" (Currie 1993: 3). He concludes that our policy has been directed at a variety of largely repressive policies including moral exhortation and punishment along with a little neglect and some attempt at treatment, but after all that we have "tried everything but improving lives" (Currie 1993: 332). He reaches this conclusion on the basis of his review of decades of research on drugs and drug policy that expose the roots of what he calls the drug crisis. We noted earlier that Cressey argued that by losing their focus on "seeking valid propositions stated in a causal framework," criminologists became "policy advisors in this repressive war on crime" (Cressey 1978: 173, 184). In that same spirit, for drug policy Currie suggests there is still hope when he writes, "The first step, then, toward a real war on drug abuse is to reopen, without apology, the question of root causes" (Currie 1993: 35). That change of direction would be facilitated by a change in the theoretical foundation on which we would build a productive research agenda that would inform a defensible policy.

Informing the discourse on drug policy

Reality is a social construction. In everyday life people construct objective facticities from subjective meanings through their decisions, actions, and interaction in relation to other people around them (Berger and Luckmann 1966). But social actors act and interact, make decisions, and define their experience to themselves and to others around them in terms of the context of their own knowledge, beliefs, attitudes, values, and interests. We all do this and we do it in the intersubjective world we share with others. Consequently, for each of us the social reality within which we live is greatly influenced by those among us who have the greatest power to impose their will on our shared social reality (Brownstein 2000; Quinney 1970). Contemporary social theorists who study this process have argued that individuals as members of society make claims about the reality of their shared social experience and social reality is constructed as the product of a competition and collaboration among claimsmakers (Best 1990, 1989; Brownstein 2000; Miller and Holstein 1993; Spector and Kitsuse 1987; Woolgar and Pawluch 1985). Joel Best has called this the "marketplace of claims" (Best 1990: 15).

Social policy is a social phenomenon so in the same way it can be viewed as a construction that is the product of a competition and collaboration taking place in a marketplace of claims. In the claims-making marketplace where policy is made are scientists and ideologues including lobbyists representing the countless interest groups that pay them to do so, politicians worrying about getting reelected to office, agents of government agencies arguing for expansion of their budget and authority, researchers making recommendations from the findings of their research, other researchers making different recommendations from the findings of their research, and any number of others pressuring the people with the power to make policy to make the policy they favor (Brownstein 2007; Denzau and Munger 1986; Ismaili 2006; Stolz 2002). Given their need as scientists to remain objective and value free, social scientists are at a disadvantage in this arena (Brownstein 2007, 1998; Ismaili 2006; Stolz 2005; Trostle et al. 1999). If researchers as social scientists are to have an impact on drug policy, they need to figure out a way to compete more successfully in the marketplace where drug policy is made. They are not the only ones with claims to make about drugs, and some of the other claimsmakers are pretty good at it.

In the effort to produce valid and reliable knowledge to inform responsible and effective policy, evidence based on science can be pretty compelling. But early in the twenty-first century, not unlike some times in earlier centuries, not everyone believes in science. Some people, for example, place their faith in religious beliefs or ideology. Some people believe knowledge and evidence about the consequences or impact of things should guide social decisions and actions, others believe decisions and actions should be guided by ideas and values. Some people think both are relevant to some degree. Science can provide us with empirical evidence and logic to explain the consequences of doing things one way or another, but not everyone thinks that matters. So even if we all sat down in good faith to talk about how to deal with drugs and the people who are involved with them, we are not necessarily going to be able to communicate let alone understand each other and make the best possible policy. Still, unless we make the effort to talk to each other we are going to be stuck with policies that do not address real problems and satisfy no one.

There are many organizations and associations around the world that are interested in drug policy. They hold lots of public forums and meetings throughout the year in cities around the world. This should be a good way to promote discourse about drug policy, but organizations and associations like this by design attract like-minded people. Several call for open debate and even promote science and evidence, but argue for a particular position with regard to drug policy. For example, the Drug Policy Alliance is concerned with compassion and human rights and health, promotes alternatives to current drug policy, and explicitly favors policies grounded in science (http://www.drugpolicy.org/). Common Sense for Drug Policy overtly expresses interest in bringing together like-minded people and educating the public about alternatives to current policies (http://www.csdp.org/cms/). The International Society for the Study of Drug Policy is a forum for open debate on drug policy that supports evidence-based policies toward the reduction of drug-related harm (http://www.issdp.org/index.php). The Criminal Justice Policy Foundation funds the National Drug Strategy Network and tells prospective supporters that due to the failure of the war on drugs it is now time to rethink drug policy (http://www.cjpf.org/drug). It is not easy to find any organizations advocating drug prohibition, but there are a few. The Freestyle Foundation (http://www.drugfreecalifornia.org/about.html) promotes substance free living and works in California with its partner association, Stars and Stripes United, an organization that supports local grassroots movements across the country to challenge "the audacity of government leaders who degrade our beloved Nation and her Founding principles" to create anti-drug use coalitions (http://www.starsandstripesunited.com/default.asp?contentID=10). There are also government agencies that express positions. For example, the US Office of National Drug Control Policy argues that some reform is needed to bring more attention to health problems, but progress has been made over the three decades of the war on drugs so a balanced approach is favored (http://www.whitehouse.gov/ondcp). The closed circle of people in a given organization can have a limiting effect on open discourse in organizational or association publications or at theoretically open meetings.

This book is not intended to tell policymakers what to do when it comes to making drug policy, or even to tell other social scientists and other scientists how to do that. Rather it is intended to identify and examine areas where open, honest, and active discourse would be of value to people who make policy related to what we call drugs, drug using, and drug involvement. Each of the next three chapters focuses on a particular area of concern and the related need for debate or discourse with special attention to how both ideology and criminological theory have guided the debate and discourse and the resultant policy. In particular, these chapters focus on how criminological theory has played a role in guiding drug policy over the past 75 years or so, notably but not only in the US, and has lead that policy in a specific direction, more often than not toward a more repressive war on drugs. Broadly, each of the three chapters is about whether or not, why, and how drugs, including the use of licit and illicit drugs and the illicit use of licit drugs, are considered a problem and if so what is the nature of the problem. Chapter 2 is about public policies that view drugs as a broad social problem of safety and health and are directed at regulating or controlling that problem. Ultimately, this becomes a discussion about the appropriate legal status of drugs, drug users, drug dealers, and anyone else involved with drugs. Relevant policies would emphasize law enforcement and prohibition. Chapter 3 is about policies that similarly view drugs as a problem but in a different way, mostly in terms of health, and are directed at managing that problem. Ultimately, this becomes a discussion about the harms experienced or not by people and communities as a result of the use, misuse, or abuse of various drugs. Relevant policies would emphasize harm reduction in terms of things like prevention, treatment, and caring. Chapter 4 is about policies concerning the proper place in society for the use of drugs and the people who use them. Ultimately, this becomes a discussion about values, and whether members of a society can agree on what drugs or when drugs or how drugs are worthy of being available for consumption by some people or by all people. In this case, theoretically, a consensus could be reached that drugs are a problem of having things or people in society that need to be removed, or that drugs are not a problem in any way for any people so the only policy would be no policy.

In each of these following chapters the discussion will consider the ideological and theoretical foundations of the direction of particular contemporary drug policies relative to the way the problem of drugs is defined and addressed. Consequently, considerable attention will be on the underlying or background assumptions that support the ideology or theory itself. Since, as noted earlier, there is already substantial evidence of the impact of ideology on drug policy, more attention will be given to theory, in particular how mainstream and critical criminological theories point drug policy in different directions.

2

THE DEBATE OVER CONTROL AND REGULATION

After World War II white people in large numbers began leaving the Bronx borough of New York City and were replaced mainly by black people and people from Puerto Rico. Official census data show that in 1990 there were 1,203,789 people living in the Bronx with more than 37 per cent classified as black and more than 43 per cent as Hispanic. During the 1970s and into the 1980s many sections of the Bronx, like some other sections of New York and sections of other cities as well, experienced increasing levels of crime, gang activity, and the use and sale of illicit drugs, particularly crack cocaine. During this period much of the Bronx also experienced a growing number of families and children living in poverty and a steady decline in the value of local real estate. For much of this time much of the Bronx was represented in the New York State Senate by Joseph Galiber.

Senator Joseph Galiber was himself an African American Bronx Democrat who served his district for almost three decades before he passed away in 1995. On April 18, 1988 he introduced Senate Bill 1918, "An Act to amend the executive law, in relation to establishing a controlled substances authority and to repeal articles 220 and 221 of the penal law, relating to controlled substances offenses and involving marijuana and article thirty-three of the public health law, relating to controlled substances." In other words, at the time when the threat and fear of crack cocaine enthralled lawmakers, law enforcers, public health officials, and the media and fully captured the public imagination, Senator Galiber was proposing that New York repeal the state laws that make the sale and possession of controlled substances illegal.

In proposing his bill the Senator was not arguing that the use, possession, or sale of substances currently controlled by law should suddenly become unregulated and uncontrolled. In a memorandum he submitted with his bill he argued that "the goal of this bill is to regulate and control the manufacture, sale, and distribution within the state of controlled substances for the purpose of fostering and promoting temperance in their consumption and respect for and obedience to law." The bill did not endorse or encourage irresponsible use of substances that could be dangerous to the user or the people around him or her. Its concern, as Senator Galiber told a reporter according to an article that appeared in the *Albany Times Union* newspaper on November 17, 1989 (page B-12), was to take the profit out of illicit drug markets and to eliminate the violence related to them. That is, his legislation was designed to regulate drug use, possession, and sales to be able to address their negative consequences for people and communities rather than to indiscriminately arrest and punish all users, possessors, and dealers.

An internal memorandum written for the Governor of New York dated December 28, 1989 and called *Analysis of S.1918* summarizes the highlights of the Galiber bill. His staff informed Governor Mario Cuomo that the Galiber bill would create a State Controlled Substances Authority made up of five members with the power to: "issue, refuse, revoke, or cancel licenses for the legal sale and manufacture of controlled substances; to fix standards of quality control, specifications, labeling and quantitative limits in the manufacture and sale of controlled substances; and to keep records on licenses granted, denied or revoked." The bill would have allowed authorized doctors or pharmacists to apply for a license for the legal sale of controlled substances, but they could not do business near a school or a place of worship and they could not sell to any person younger than 21 years of age.

The bill was submitted by Senator Galiber without the support of any of his colleagues in the State Senate. Besides having no support from his Senate colleagues, the 1989 memorandum prepared for the Governor by his staff was critical of every aspect of the bill and resulted in a negative response from the Governor's office. The memo concluded:

> Senate Bill 1918 would dramatically increase drug abuse since it would open the gateway to obtaining drugs by legal means. In this sense, the State would be facilitating drug abuse, without any checks to prevent disastrous health effects from overdose and multi-substance dependency, or associated social effects. Individuals who would not otherwise have used drugs because of legal sanctions with attendant social standards would use and abuse them. More children and more pregnant women would find drugs accessible and fewer addicts would turn to treatment without the leverage of the criminal justice system.

There was no scientific evidence included in the memo to support any of these claims, because none existed (in fact, the body of relevant research and analytical evidence was growing at the time, but it did not support the arguments being made in the memo). There were public hearings held around the state in 1988 and 1989 at which Senator Galiber argued, according to the *Albany Times Union* article of November 17, 1989, that his goal was "to get people thinking about the other ways of slowing the spread of dangerous drugs to people."

Ultimately, that was the underlying problem faced by Galiber and others who thought about drugs and their use and misuse the way he thought about them. At the time we knew something but not everything about how illicit drug use spread and something about health problems associated with the misuse of drugs; we knew less about how drugs, licit or illicit, were related to crime and violence. Nonetheless, public officials and private citizens alike believed they knew. At a time in the US when crime and illicit drug use seemed to be spreading and people and communities were deeply concerned, it was hard to have an open discussion about what the problem was or even if there was a problem, and how it might be addressed to best deal with any negative personal or social consequences there might be. There was no support for any discussion about controlled substances that even hinted at the possibility of changing the way things were being done. Legalization was a dirty word and any attempt to start a conversation about regulation was considered an appeal to legalize.

Not everything that people do is controlled by law. Not every substance that people consume is regulated by law. But the idea that there should be laws regulating what substances people can and cannot consume has become immutable. In this chapter we consider the social, cultural, and historical context in which regulations have evolved to control what substances should or should not be consumed by people and when, where, and why they should be consumed. Then we consider the assumptions behind the ideology and theory that guided the actions and decisions that supported the formulation of policies for controlling drug use and involvement.

Social, cultural, and historical context

For the first five years that Joseph Galiber was a State Senator, the Governor of New York was Nelson Rockefeller. Governor Rockefeller had a notable and sometimes noble impact on Albany and New York, and eventually through various political appointments also had some influence on the nation. But of all the things he ever did or did not do, and some were quite impressive, one ignominious accomplishment that will forever bear his name is what is commonly called "Rockefeller's Drug Law." Around the time this law was passed the Association of the Bar of the City of New York called it "the nation's toughest drug law" (Joint Committee on New York Drug Law Evaluation 1977). It was against the backdrop of that piece of legislation that Joseph Galiber introduced his bill to the New York State Senate to change the state's drugs laws.

Through the 1960s state policy in New York was to divert low-level illicit drug users to treatment and to focus the attention of the justice system on major traffickers. By the early 1970s an increasing number of accidental drug-related deaths in the state encouraged the Governor with the State Legislature to introduce a new approach. The result was the passage of Rockefeller's Drug Law, which was largely in place with periodic amendments from 1973 when it was initially passed until it was substantially reformed in 2009 (Office of Justice Research and Performance 2010a, 2010b). Essentially, under the Law there were mandatory minimum prison sentences for minor drug offenders, mandatory indeterminate sentences for more serious felony offenders, and limits on plea bargaining, especially for second felony offenders.

From the passage of the Rockefeller Drug Law through the time Senator Galiber proposed his bill the numbers of people in New York arrested, prosecuted, and sentenced to prison for drug offending, major and minor, grew dramatically. A report by the New York State Division of Criminal Justice Services (DCJS), the agency that maintains criminal history records for all offenders in the state, reported that from 1983 to 1987, just before Senate Bill 1918 was first introduced, the annual number of felony and misdemeanor drug arrests in the state doubled from 53,769 to 106,658, with felony drug arrests accounting for almost two-thirds of the total increase of all felony arrests in the state during the period (Ross and Cohen 1988: 1). In 1987 in New York of all people arrested on a felony drug charge, 49 per cent were black and 21 per cent were Hispanic (Ross and Cohen 1988: 7). During those same years the proportion of felony drug arrests in the state that were prosecuted in the upper court as more serious offenses increased from 35 per cent to 51 per cent, the number of convictions from both misdemeanor and felony arrests rose 78 per cent (to 59,605), and the number of people convicted of a drug charge who were then sentenced to incarceration increased by 170 per cent to 39,908 (Ross and Cohen 1988: 12–14). This helps to explain the findings of a report in 1991 by the state corrections agency that found, "In the early 1980s, drug offenders accounted for roughly 10% of all new court commitments to the New York State Department of Correctional Services (DOCS). The proportion of drug offenders in the commitment population rose steadily from 1984 to 1990, when 46.7% of all new court commitments were admitted for drug offenses" (Humphrey 1991: 1). Thus by the time Senator Galiber suggested that New York might want to reconsider the aggressive drug policy in the state, the number of people committed to state prisons for drug offenses exceeded the number of people committed for any other offense, including all violent offenses.

New York was not the only state getting tough on people who possessed, used, or sold drugs classified as illegal during the last decades of the twentieth century. Around that time a report by the National Council on Crime and Delinquency concluded that the outcome of contemporary drug policy in the US would be to "overwhelm the nation's correctional systems over the next five years" (Austin and McVey 1989: 1). Using official statistics maintained by the federal Bureau of Justice Statistics

(BJS), Blumstein and Beck reported that the number of people in prison for one of six serious crimes (murder, robbery, aggravated assault, burglary, drugs, and sexual assaults) increased by 268 per cent from 234,000 people in 1980 to 860,000 in 1996 (Blumstein and Beck 1999: 20). They found that inmates sentenced to prison for drug offenses accounted for the largest part of the increase, a 45 per cent increase in drug offenders in prison, or 33 per cent of the total growth in the level of incarceration (Blumstein and Beck 1999: 21–22).

Across the US the direction of drug policy increasingly focused on getting tough on drugs through control and regulation. As noted earlier, in 1971 President Richard Nixon declared war on drugs, and in 1982 President Ronald Reagan reaffirmed that declaration (Inciardi 2007; Weisheit 1990; Wisotsky 1986). Then in 1989 President George H.W. Bush and the US Congress saw the need to have a strategy to fight the war so the Office of National Drug Control Policy (ONDCP) was established as part of the Executive Office of the President. William Bennett was named its first director. The war was on. In the first annual strategy Bennett wrote, "In the teeth of a crisis—especially one which for so long appeared to spiral wildly out of control—we naturally look for villains. We need not look far; there are plenty of them. Anyone who sells drugs—and (to a great if poorly understood extent) anyone who uses them—is involved in an international criminal enterprise that is killing thousands of Americans each year" (ONDCP 1989: 7). From the beginning of the ONDCP in 1989 and in every year since, the Office has issued a strategy report, and every report has demonstrated through both its narrative and its detailed budgetary proposals that the most important aspect of the drug strategy in the US is control, with funding for enforcement and interdiction regularly exceeding funding for prevention and treatment (http://www.whitehouse.gov/ondcp/2012-national-drug-control-strategy). From the start not everyone has agreed with this approach to drugs (Curtis 1989), but in the US government throughout this period the ONDCP and the White House were not alone in favoring a get tough policy on drugs. Right after the first ONDCP strategy was released the Office of the Attorney General (1989) and the US Congress (Biden 1990) both issued reports that effectively supported the ONDCP strategy.

Other nations more concerned with the consequences of drug use, misuse, or distribution rather than the indiscriminate control of drugs did not all necessarily support the get tough drug policy taking hold in the US (Cohen 1996; Inciardi and Harrison 2000; MacCoun and Reuter 1997; Riley *et al.* 1999). But on the international level during this period nations of the world were meeting through the United Nations and negotiating the agreements that became the three UN Conventions. As noted earlier, the first (United Nations 1961) consolidated earlier multinational treaties, the second (United Nations 1971) extended international control to synthetic psychotropic substances, and the third (United Nations 1988) focused on international drug trafficking. Together they brought attention on the international level to controlling the supply of drugs with an emphasis on prohibition and criminalization (Bewley-Taylor 2003; Room and Reuter 2011). In 2001 a report to the Canadian Parliament blamed the power of more developed nations, notably the US, over less developed nations for the focus on controlling the drug trade rather than helping people and communities that were having problems dealing with drugs (Sinha 2001).

Theoretical foundations

When the intent of drug policy is to control or regulate the use and distribution of all drugs or particular drugs and all people or particular people who use them in all or particular circumstances, then the strategy predictably is both punitive and coercive emphasizing: (1) prohibition and enforcement to limit the supply of drugs available for unsanctioned purposes or by unauthorized people, or (2) prevention and treatment to limit the demand for drugs among users and potential users (cf. Dobkin and Nicosia 2009; Kleiman 1992; Kleiman *et al.* 2011; Newcomb 1992; Reuter 1992). This has been and continues to be the focus of drug policy under the flag of the war on drugs in the US. In the heat of battle, William Bennett, the first director of the Office of National Drug Control Policy of the Executive Office of the President, issued the following statement in his second annual *National Drug Control Strategy* report: "it is the policy of the United States to disrupt, dismantle, and ultimately destroy the illegal market for drugs" (ONDCP 1990: 1). With those words he clearly framed the national drug policy as a policy of control and regulation. In 2012 President Barack Obama introduced the annual drug strategy report by announcing that in the US drug policy would take a more balanced approach (ONDCP 2012a: iii). In the same report in the proposed budget for spending on drug initiatives in the next fiscal year, 59 per cent of proposed spending was directed to supply side efforts (domestic law enforcement, interdiction, and international programs) with 41 per cent for demand side efforts (prevention, treatment), a ratio that has remained constant for the past several years (ONDCP 2012b: 13). In either case, however, the policy essentially would be the same. On the supply side the policy follows a moral model distinguishing good behavior from bad behavior and devoting resources to control the bad behavior; on the demand side the policy follows a medical model viewing drug users as suffering from a biological or genetic disorder and devoting resources to control the drug use of these sick people (Marlatt 1996). Either way, the goal is to control or regulate the behavior or activity of people involved with drugs.

Any policy position starts with assumptions about human nature, the nature of social reality, and accepted criteria for having confidence in what is known and how it is known. As discussed earlier, assumptions are untested or unverifiable propositions based on taken for granted beliefs, values, or attitudes that are used to fill the gaps in our knowledge about a phenomenon so that we can recognize and comprehend that phenomenon in our experience with other people around us as logical and coherent (cf. Fuhrman 1989; Gouldner 1970). In terms of the relationship between policy and underlying assumptions, Schneider and Ingram wrote, "public policy almost always attempts to get people to do things that they might not otherwise do; or it enables people to do things that they might not have done otherwise. For policies to have the intended impacts on society, a large number of people in different situations must make decisions and take actions in concert with policy objectives" (Schneider and Ingram 1990: 513). To that end a drug policy, for example, would need to have an appreciation for how people will behave and confidence in the knowledge that they will behave that way. So to believe that a drug policy emphasizing control and regulation will be successful in reducing or eliminating whatever problems are believed to be associated with drugs, drug using, or the distribution of drugs, certain assumptions need to be made about how people will behave in response to that policy.

In that ideology by definition advocates a position on the basis of knowledge supported by facts that are reputed but not necessarily verified (cf. Gauchat 2012; Leiss 1975), ideologically it would not be difficult to construct a logical and coherent drug policy favoring any position, including control or regulation. Theory is part of the scientific process so requires that what is accepted as known be validated through a process of testing and verification through which new knowledge is confirmed and discredited knowledge is discarded (cf. Kuhn 1977; Popper 1959). Nonetheless, as new knowledge is being confirmed and discredited knowledge discarded, the gaps left by what is not known are filled by assumptions.

To accept that control or regulation are appropriate policy responses to drugs requires a belief that drugs pose a problem or problems that can be addressed by control or regulation. That is, first it is necessary to accept that people involved with drugs do pose a threat to social order, in particular in terms of public safety and public health, and that the problem can be addressed by controlling or regulating the behavior or activity of the people involved. Official criminal justice records in the US and the UK, for example, suggest that lots of people who get caught up in the nets of things like arrest, conviction, and incarceration are involved with drugs, and that lots of people involved with drugs get into trouble (Chaplin et al. 2011; FBI 2011; National Institute of Justice 2003; ONDCP 2011; Smith and Flatley 2011). And there are people who use drugs in ways that are detrimental to their own health or to the health of others around them, as in the case of things like addiction, overdose, diseases or injuries related to certain types of drug use, or the spread of disease among drug users (Berridge and Bourne 2005; Des Jarlais 1996; SAMHSA 2012, 2011).

But at the same time there are lots of people who are involved with drugs that are prescribed by medical personnel or are sold to anyone walking into a retail outlet that openly displays a wide variety of drugs for public consumption. Typically, these people do not disrupt the lives of others around them and in fact it is possible and even intended that their use of drugs makes them even less disruptive than they would otherwise have been without the drugs. And there are people who use various drugs for recreational or personal or social purposes that may or may not be legally authorized for any purpose, but despite their use of such drugs, licit and illicit, these people do not engage in disruptive behavior (Goode 2012; Zinberg 1984). That is, sometimes and in some settings drug involvement is normal and is not a problem for individuals or society.

So how can we justify a drug policy intended to broadly and all-inclusively control or regulate drug use and drug involvement? Why would we set abstinence as a policy goal? More than a century ago Edward Ross, a pioneering American sociologist, defined social control as the "levers which set in motion the social checks or stimuli that hold a man back or push him on" (Ross 1901: 77). For Ross these levers were grounded in moral or ethical standards and by the middle of the twentieth century his idea of social control came to be accepted by sociologists as "the various means used by a society to bring its recalcitrant members back into line" (Berger 1963: 68). In that sense a policy of control would make sense assuming we believe that any drug using or drug distribution or any type of involvement with drugs deemed unauthorized or illegal is the behavior of recalcitrant members of society engaged in immoral or unethical acts that disrupt society and place other people at risk. During the middle of the twentieth century a number of criminological theories built around this assumption directly or indirectly supported a control-oriented drug policy.

Early mainstream criminological theories of social control explained deviant behavior in terms of why people do or do not conform to social norms, and in particular laws (Reckless 1961; Reiss 1951; Sykes and Matza 1957). Perhaps of greatest influence, Hirschi focused on delinquency and argued that for young people to learn to conform they needed to be bonded to society through their relationships with others while having a stake in the social order, a commitment to and involvement with conventional activity, and a belief in moral order and law (Hirschi 1969). Later with Gottfredson he shifted his focus from social control through bonding to the notion of self-control, arguing that youth with low self-control will more likely engage in criminal activity (Gottfredson and Hirschi 1990). Underlying these mainstream theories emphasizing the need for control is the Hobbesian assumption that people are basically evil and need to be controlled in order to conform to social norms and thereby to be able to live among other people in a civil society (Bohm and Vogel 2011).

A related mainstream criminological theory that supports a control-oriented drug policy suggests that when social norms break down, a condition that is called anomie (Durkheim 1933), individuals become dissociated from society and consequently violations of the social order occur. Society is comprised of routine patterns of behavior in the form of social norms that present themselves to us through social institutions that then act in relation to us as regulatory patterns of behavior (cf. Berger 1963). In other words, when social institutions are recognized by individuals as an external and objective reality we give them authority to coerce us to behave in normative ways. But when the social structure made up of these institutions disassembles or disintegrates then the ability of the institutions to regulate our behavior is diminished. Starting in the early twentieth century social disorganization theorists, for example, proposed a social ecological perspective arguing that individuals were not necessarily different in terms of their predisposition for deviant or criminal behavior but rather the explanation for why some engaged in deviance or crime and others did not was found in the characteristics of the neighborhood where they lived (Shaw and McKay 1942). Other theorists focused directly on anomie and argued that deviance or crime could be explained by the strain placed on individuals given the discrepancy between the social rewards they believed should be attainable and those that actually were (Cohen 1955; Cloward and Ohlin 1960; Merton 1938).

In the late nineteenth century criminological theorists were influenced by the development of biological positivism leading them to focus on criminals rather than crime to discover underlying causes for observed criminal behavior (Bernard *et al.* 2002). Prominent among them was Cesare Lombroso who studied the physical characteristics of Italian prisoners comparing them to those of Italian soldiers and concluding that the physical differences he observed could explain criminal behavior (Lombroso-Ferrero and Savitz 1972). While not so deterministic, in that same tradition mainstream criminological theorists more recently have argued that deviant or disruptive behavior can be explained independently or in interaction with social forces or conditions in terms of biological or psychological traits considering things like body type, intelligence, temperament, hormones, or genetics (Denno 1988; Fishbein 1990; Wilson and Herrnstein 1985). In terms of drugs, contemporary researchers and theorists have been devoting considerable time and energy to finding a way to explain drug use behavior in terms of the human brain (Koob and

Volkow 2010). The point is that these theories, like the social control theories and social disorganization theories, view the problem in terms of the behavior or actions of social actors who can be fixed by some form of intervention.

In terms of drug policy, these mainstream theories lead to the conclusion that the appropriate response to individual involvement with drugs would be to correct the actions of these recalcitrant individuals. Given that assumption, control or regulation would make sense. If the behavior is deemed antisocial then the policy could be to introduce initiatives and programs that intervene through law enforcement, the courts, and correctional institutions. If the behavior is deemed a health risk to people then the policy could be to introduce initiatives and programs that intervene by treating people who use drugs or preventing others from using them. But in terms of drug policy, a shortcoming of these mainstream theories is that they focus on individual behavior and social activity, define it as negative or positive, and then place responsibility for that activity and any social consequences related to it on the social actor. For drug policy in particular there is the added problem that drug involvement is not always a social problem or even a problem for the user. Using drugs or selling drugs is sometimes socially acceptable and sometimes legally prescribed. Using drugs or selling them to people who need them may even benefit the individual user and others around him or her. So being involved with drugs is not by itself necessarily a bad thing for society or for individuals (cf. Currie 1993; Lindesmith 1938, 1973; Nadelmann 1989, 2007; Trebach 1982; Weil 1972; Zinberg 1984).

Alternative directions and questions to consider

On July 16, 2012 Cory Booker, the Mayor of the city of Newark, New Jersey, signed on to Reddit (http://www.reddit.com/search?q=Cory+Booker+drugs (accessed July 18, 2012)), a social news website where participants post articles and comments so other participants on the site can read them and vote to determine their importance relative to other posts. Not only did Mayor Booker's post get lots of attention on the site, newspapers around the country picked it up and reported what he said and how he said it. The gist of his post was that the war on drugs is ineffective. He was quoted as saying, "My police in Newark are involved in an almost ridiculous game of arresting the same people over and over again and when you talk to these men they have little belief that there is help or hope for them to break out of this cycle." Most of what he proposed as an alternative to what he called the drug arrests "game" were criminal justice modifications (e.g. reentry programs, court reforms) or social or legal support services (e.g. jobs, legal aid, treatment). So the position he took was not really outside of the control and regulation model of drug policy. But with his leap into cyberspace to talk about drug policy he did expose some of the cracks in the control or regulation canon.

Mainstream criminological theories like control theory and social disorganization theory as well as biological positivism have supported the advancement of a one-dimensional and linear drug policy focused on controlling the supply of or demand for drugs or both. They make it possible for policymakers to view drug policy as if the question is simply how to control or regulate the supply of drugs with enforcement or interdiction strategies or the demand for drugs with treatment or prevention strategies. These two approaches are not mutually exclusive as each is a different side of the same war on drugs with the shared goal of trying to reduce the overall consumption of particular drugs, the first by trying to control the availability of those drugs or the settings in which drugs can be used and the latter by trying to control the interest that people have or might have in the use of these drugs or of any drugs outside of approved settings or contexts (Goldstein 2001: 294). So the question is not simply whether all drugs or any drugs should be prohibited or made legal or where or when it should be legitimate to use drugs. This is a false issue, or what Avram Goldstein calls a "false dichotomy" (Goldstein 2001: 293). Drugs are not just a single phenomenon and the place of drugs in our society is much more complicated than any single policy to control or regulate them or the people involved with them could possibly address.

Contemporary critical criminological theory offers an opportunity to move drug policy in a direction that recognizes and acknowledges the complexity of drug use and drug involvement in society. For example, in advocating for a peacemaking criminology Hal Pepinsky wrote, "Rather than doing things to offenders, peacemaking requires us to do things with offenders and others" (Pepinsky 1991: 96). He observed that punitive measures in social relations are essentially an exercise through which those with power maintain control over those who do not have power, and argued that in a truly democratic society all people who are involved in a social interaction have a unique perspective on the interaction and a stake in its outcome, so all should participate in making decisions about its resolution (Pepinsky 1991, 1987, 1986; Pepinsky and Jesilow 1984; Pepinsky and Quinney 1991). He based his argument on the notion of "participatory justice" introduced by Nils Christie who recognized peace in social relations as a moral alternative to war when he wrote, "imposing punishment within the institution of law means the inflicting of pain, intended as pain. This is an activity which often comes into dissonance to esteemed values such as kindness and forgiveness" (Christie 1981: 5). Peacemaking criminology then is about recognizing the decency and interconnectedness of people and their need to be kind to each other and forgiving of each other.

In terms of drug policy, during the late twentieth century there was some attention among critics of the war on drugs to making peace with the people involved with those drugs not deemed by the wider society to be legitimate and the people involved with legitimate drugs in unapproved settings and ways (Alexander 1990; Anderson 1981; Brownstein 1992, 1990; Reinarman and Levine 1990; Trebach 1986; Weisheit 1990; Wisotsky 1986). The notion of war is based on punitive measures to control the supply of drugs and coercive measures to control the use of drugs. The notion of peace would end the war and instead focus on working with people involved with drugs to find resolutions to any problems associated with drugs and to maximize the advantages gained by people and communities from drugs. In other words, it would not separate drugs or people distributing or using drugs in terms of good guys (e.g. medical and healthcare authorized providers; users of prescribed drugs) and bad guys (e.g. dealers of illicit drugs; users of illicit drugs). A peacemaking approach would be more inclusive and responsive. It would shift the focus of drug policy away from programs meant to control or regulate the actions and behavior of people who are involved with unapproved drugs, or people who are involved with approved drugs but in unapproved ways. It would direct attention toward programs that serve the legitimate needs of all and any people for drugs that enhance rather than diminish personal and public health, safety, and fulfillment (Brownstein 1990: 118).

As Martin Schwartz and Suzanne Hatty wrote, critical criminology includes "an intellectual space in which a broad variety of people could come together to think through issues related to power, crime and punishment. ... All critical theorists share in common a concern with class, or at least the economic structure of society, and the manner in which the inequalities of modern capitalist society influence crime" (Schwartz and Hatty 2003: x). Thus for critical criminological theory in general the vision of a more just and humane society is thwarted by how power is used by those who have it to control the distribution of societal resources. Consequently, contemporary critical criminological theorists are concerned not only with class but also with race and gender and their intersections in social life particularly as they relate to identity and experience (Bohm and Vogel 2011; Curran and Renzetti 2001; Schwartz and Hatty 2003). The challenge then for peacemaking criminological theory in relation to the war on drugs is to help direct society toward a world in which all people are recognized as inherently decent and equally deserving of the opportunity to fully share in the resources of society that would allow them the greatest chance for a healthy, safe, and fulfilled life.

The problem of power for drug policy is not only a concern in terms of the distribution of tangible resources in society, but also in terms of the construction of social reality. Postmodern and poststructural criminological theorists are concerned with the construction of knowledge and in particular the use of language to create hierarchy and domination in criminal justice institutions and processes (Arrigo and Bernard 1997). They raise questions such as why some actions or behaviors come to be defined as crime or criminal and others not. This line of questioning has specific application for drug policy and the central role of social construction and power in making policies favoring control and regulation (Welch et al. 1998). In the nineteenth century the classical sociologist Max Weber argued that social action is the basic unit of society and defined it as "all human behavior when and in so far as the acting individual attaches subjective meaning to it" (Weber 1947: 88). More recently Alfred Schutz wrote from a phenomenological perspective, "Strictly speaking, there are no such thing as facts, pure and simple" (Schutz 1962: 5). The point is that social action or behavior takes on the meaning we intersubjectively assign to it.

Recognizing that reality is a social construction (Berger and Luckmann 1966), social constructionist theorists think about policy-making as a process of competition and collaboration among advocates making a multiplicity of claims about the nature and dynamics of social reality (Brownstein 2007). Writing about the construction of social problems, this is what Joel Best called the "marketplace of claims" (Best 1990). In the case of drug policy in the US, for example, the advocates for a policy of control and regulation have been winning this competition (cf. Currie 1993; Walker 2011). The reason for this is not so obvious given what we know about drugs and their impact on public health and safety from the extant body of scientific knowledge. The social constructionist perspective helps us to understand this in terms of how power relations and social divisions can shape interpretations of measured outcomes of the control policy to support the claims of the drug warriors. For example, considering the period in the US when crack cocaine spurred a great public concern about drugs, Elliott Currie wrote:

> Even many who support the thrust of our present drug policies would acknowledge that the drug crisis among "hard-core" users in the more marginal populations is understated by conventional statistics, and that it has proven remarkably resistant to the conventional tools of the drug war. But they would argue that the declines in *middle*-class drug use prove that the drug war is "on the right track," and that if we only redoubled our efforts we could make it work against the admittedly tougher situation in the inner cities as well.
>
> *(Currie 1993: 30)*

He went on to say, "The trouble with that view is that the conventional drug war had virtually nothing to do with the declines in drug use among the better-off, for it was never *fought* against their drug use" (Currie 1993: 30). That is, the war on drugs and the control policy on which it is based was being fought in one way (against select groups of people distinguished by characteristics like race and class) and its success interpreted in another way (as if it was equally directed at all people).

The purpose of this chapter is not necessarily to argue that an effective drug policy would not include any elements of control or regulation.

Whatever good they do, for some people and in some cases drugs do have negative consequences for the health and safety of individuals and their communities. The point rather is that having drugs in society is not a simple matter and a single-minded policy cannot successfully maximize the positive and minimize the negative ways that what we call drugs can and should be part of our ongoing social experience. And to the extent that we might include control or regulation strategies as part of an overall policy there are a number of questions that we would need to seriously consider. For example: To what extent do drugs benefit and to what extent are drugs a problem for the people involved with them or for the people around them? If they are a problem, does it make sense that any or all drugs be prohibited, and how can we identify particular drugs that could or should be prohibited or available on a limited basis? If there are drugs that should be prohibited or their availability limited, how do we decide which drugs, under what circumstances, who should have access to them, and who should not? And if we decide that we need to have regulations or controls, what regulations or controls are appropriate or necessary to make sure that only the approved drugs are used only by the approved people in only the approved circumstances? As a democratic society, how do we make sure that all people are being treated fairly and equally when we make the distinctions about who can use what drugs and when they can use them? Is it even possible and is it fair to try to control behavior? Given human nature and the nature of society, to what extent is it even possible for us to make reasonable decisions and set realistic policies that would control the behavior of people who seek to use unapproved drugs or approved drugs in unapproved circumstances or to be involved with drugs in unapproved ways? With all that has been written and all the arguments that have been made, we still need to have the debate that would address questions like these before we can know when and how to include control and regulation in an overall drug policy.

3
THE DEBATE OVER MANAGEMENT

A new law took effect in the Netherlands on January 1, 2012. Effective from that date, the law permits the sale of cannabis to residents of the Netherlands while banning sale to tourists even in the coffee shops that for decades have been selling to residents and tourists alike. Newspapers around the world saw humor in this development. On April 28, 2012 *The Sydney Morning Herald* ran the headline, "Dutch laws set to weed out stoned tourists," and that same day the headline in the *New York Post* read, "End of the Dutch pot party." On May 1 the *London Free Press* reported, "Protestors get puffy about Dutch pot ban." Certainly tourists travel to the Netherlands to see the museums with their great works of the Dutch masters and to ride boats on the canals in Amsterdam or travel through the countryside looking for tulips and windmills. But the open sale of cannabis in the local coffee shops has long been an important part of a major tourist industry. So not only tourists but also owners of the coffee shops and advocates of the open sale and use of marijuana did not think the foreign headlines were funny. Perhaps any other place in the world this would have gone with little notice, but not in the Netherlands.

Given its treaty obligations as part of an international community, officially neither the sale nor possession of cannabis is legal in the

Netherlands. But for years the Dutch have practiced a tradition called *gedoogbeleid*, what MacCoun and Reuter define as "the formal, systematic application of discretion" (MacCoun and Reuter 1997: 48). In practice, enforcement efforts against large scale suppliers of cannabis have been aggressive while possession of smaller amounts by users has been tolerated. In 1976 the Dutch implemented "a policy of nonenforcement for violations involving possession or sale of up to 30g of cannabis," reducing that level to five grams in 1995 in response to both international and domestic concerns but not abandoning the policy (MacCoun and Reuter 1997: 48). Under this policy specific guidelines were established to allow coffee shop owners involved in the cannabis business to avoid prosecution (do not advertise, do not sell hard drugs to anyone or any drugs to minors, do not take advantage of the established threshold for sales, and do not cause any public disturbances) and the number of such establishments increased over time (MacCoun and Reuter 1997: 49).

The political roots of the Dutch policy toward cannabis can be traced back to the middle of the twentieth century. In the late 1960s in the midst of worldwide social upheaval and faced with limited knowledge but a lot of fear involving drugs like cannabis, two commissions were established in the Netherlands to address the problem. In 1968 the National Federation of Mental Health Organizations commissioned a panel of experts including "law enforcement officials, alcohol treatment experts, psychiatrists, a drug use researcher and a sociologist" chaired by a criminal law professor, Louk Hulsman (Cohen 1996). They concluded that in the long run the appropriate policy would be full decriminalization recommending that the movement toward decriminalization should be a gradual process; in the short run the Commission recommended removing the use and possession of small amounts of cannabis from the criminal law and providing adequate treatment for people who need it (Cohen 1996). That same year a State Commission was established by the Under Secretary of Health to be chaired by the Chief Inspector of Mental Health, Pieter Baan, and including some of the same people as were serving on the Hulsman Commission. The Baan Commission covered a broad range of topics involving drugs and drug using, including for example the epidemiology of drug use in the Netherlands and relative risks of use, and concluded that criminal law is inadequate for dealing with drug users and proposed complete decriminalization as a policy goal (Cohen 1996). Effectively, the two Commission reports shifted attention from a criminal justice to a tolerance and treatment approach for dealing with people involved with drugs, particularly marijuana.

The reasoning behind the Dutch policy was that "this system of quasi-legal commercial availability not only avoids excessive punishment of casual users, but also weakens the linkage between soft- and hard-drug markets" (MacCoun and Reuter 1997: 49). As described in a recent report by the Netherlands National Drug Monitor to the European Monitoring Centre for Drugs and Drug Addiction (2011), the legal framework for national drug policy in the Netherlands includes the following four main objectives (van Laar *et al.* 2011: 15):

To prevent drug use and to treat and rehabilitate drug users
To reduce harm to users
To diminish public nuisance by drug users (the disturbance of public order and safety in the neighbourhood)
To combat the production and trafficking of drugs

The report goes on to say that the "primary aim of Dutch drug policy is focused on health protection and health risk reduction" adding that "the enforcement of relevant laws has also special attention" (van Laar *et al.* 2011: 15). Reports to the European Monitoring Centre are submitted annually, and the same list of objectives appeared in earlier reports from the Netherlands.

The drug policy in the Netherlands emphasizing harm reduction over criminal law enforcement may change with the new center-right government under Prime Minister Mark Rutte taking office at the start of 2012. The new law restricting sale of cannabis only to residents may be the start. But for our purpose here the important point is the idea that there is a rationale for arguing that focusing on how, when, and why the use or distribution of drugs might or might not be harmful to people and their communities can serve as a basis for drug policy. The issue is whether or not and how open and honest discussion about the viability and reasonableness of such a policy can continue. If we permit various substances to be used in approved ways, can we manage those personal and social harms that may arise?

Social, cultural, and historical context

An article in 1929 in a now defunct magazine, *The Literary Digest*, was called "Government Farms for Drug Addicts." It reported on a public notice broadcast over the radio by the Surgeon General of the United States Public Health Service. In the US at the start of the Great Depression on behalf of newly created Public Health narcotics division, the federal government recognizing that drug users who needed treatment were not getting it proposed to send those who committed crimes or submitted themselves voluntarily to farms where they could work and be given treatment (Literary Digest 1929: 28). The Depression was followed by World War II and over the years things changed. So different from what happened in the Netherlands, in the US the seeds of a harm reduction policy were planted but never sown.

Arguably, the contemporary roots of the notion of harm reduction as a drug policy may be traced to the UK in 1926 after the release of *The Report of the Departmental Committee on Morphine and Heroin*, which began a period of 40 years during which the medical profession regulated the distribution of opioid supplies in the UK (Bennett 1988: 299). By the end of the twentieth century harm reduction had its own journal, *Harm Reduction Journal* (http://www.harmreductionjournal.com/), and its own association, Harm Reduction International (http://www.ihra.net/about) with its own annual meeting. At the start of the twenty-first century, especially in response to the spread of AIDS during the previous decades, the approach has had considerable support in various forms in a number of European nations (Riley and O'Hare 2000).

So while the US spent the late twentieth century fighting the war on drugs, in many other parts of the world there were questions being asked about how to reduce the harm related to drugs. Harm reduction as a policy is a public health approach rather than a criminal justice approach toward drugs and drug-related issues and asks questions about how to best address and manage the personal and social harms associated with drug use in particular (DuPont and Voth 1995; Inciardi and Harrison 2000; Lindesmith 1957; Riley *et al.* 1999; Riley and O'Hare 2000). Arguably, if you consider violence a public health issue then harm reduction might also be relevant for managing drug dealing or distribution, but the focus is on users and not dealers. Specifically, it is "a public-health approach to dealing with drug-related issues that places first priority on reducing the negative consequences of drug use rather than on eliminating drug use or ensuring abstinence" (Riley et al. 1999: 10). It is grounded in principles of pragmatism and humanism, focuses on the harmful consequences of drug using and on balancing the costs and benefits of relevant decisions and actions, and places the greatest emphasis on meeting immediate needs (Hurley et al. 1997; Riley et al. 1999: 10–11).

Over the years harm reduction policies with their public health focus have resulted in a wide variety of programs designed to help people being harmed by their personal drug use to deal with their problem. For example, methadone maintenance programs have been used to stabilize and detoxify heroin users with some success not only in treating the harm of drug using for the individual but also bringing the user back into the community (Ball and Ross 1991; Joseph et al. 2000; Riley et al. 1999). Though not necessarily thought of in terms of harm reduction, methadone maintenance even achieved some popularity in the US in the 1960s (Riley et al. 1999: 13), before the war on drugs was declared. Similarly, needle or syringe exchange programs have been introduced in various communities around the world including the US to give drug users the opportunity to exchange used needles for new ones to reduce the threat of infection (Riley and O'Hare 2000).

In terms of drug treatment, during the late twentieth century in the US while the drug war was raging there was nonetheless some attention to treating people having personal and social problems associated with drugs and people having health problems related to drug use. Resources were made available for these efforts, but not to the extent that they were made available for the war effort (ONDCP 1989, 2012a). Each year in the US the Substance Abuse and Mental Health Services Administration (SAMHSA) of the US Department of Health and Human Services collects self-report survey data from approximately 67,500 people aged 12 and older for its National Survey on Drug Use and Health (NSDUH). For 2010 the NSDUH estimated that 22.6 million Americans aged 12 or older recently had used an illicit substance or had used one during the month prior to their participation in the survey, and 22.1 million people in the US (almost 9 per cent of the population aged 12 or older) could be classified with substance dependence or abuse in the past year (SAMHSA 2011). These numbers reportedly had been stable over the previous few years, but from 2002 to 2006 the number of people receiving substance abuse specialty treatment increased from 2.3 to 2.6 million (SAMHSA 2011). Unfortunately, the NSDUH report also found that in 2010 in the US there were 4.1 million people aged 12 or older who received treatment for drug or alcohol abuse and 20.5 million who were classified as in need of substance abuse treatment but did not receive it (SAMHSA 2011).

Needle exchange, a program to reduce harm for injection drug users by making available sterile needles and syringes for each injection to avoid the spread of infection, has had some popularity in other nations and there is some evidence that these programs may help manage the harm related to indiscriminate needle injection users of illicit substances without increasing the level of drug using in a community (Des Jarlais 2000; Hurley *et al.* 1997; Lurie *et al.* 1993). Explaining the logic behind needle exchange the US Centers for Disease Control and Prevention (CDC) in an issue of its regular weekly report wrote, "Syringe exchange programs (SEPs) provide free sterile syringes and collect used syringes from injection-drug users (IDUs) to reduce transmission of bloodborne pathogens, including human immunodeficiency virus (HIV), hepatitis B virus, and hepatitis C virus (HCV)" (CDC 2010: 1488). Then indicating that in 2009 there were 184 SEPs "known to be operating in 36 states, the District of Columbia (DC), and Puerto Rico," the report noted, "in 2008, the number of SEPs and the number of syringes exchanged remained similar to recent years, in contrast to a period of rapid growth from the mid-1990s through the early 2000s" (CDC 2010: 1488, 1489).

During this time there clearly has been and remains some support in the US for needle exchange. But programs are not extended to all people in all states and there has been strong opposition to them even in the federal government. Notably, despite global experience and scientific evidence suggesting that SEPs provide important public health benefits with limited risk of expanding the use of illicit drugs, a ban on federal funding for syringe or needle exchange programs was put into place by the Congress of the United States in the 1980s (General Accounting Office 1993; Hantman 1995) and after being repealed in 2009 the Congress voted to reinstate it for fiscal year 2012 (Barr 2011).

Arguably, in the US politics plays an important role in policy decisions and actions related to public health. Based on his extensive research in the area and his participation in several National Academy of Science panels on needle exchange and the US National Commission on AIDS, Don Des Jarlais has suggested, "almost 15 years' worth of data on needle exchange ... have led to changes in the positions of both original opponents and original proponents of the practice" (Des Jarlais 2000: 1393). His argument is that some interested parties are moved by the developing scientific evidence and others in the face of scientific evidence by the symbolic meaning of needle exchange (Des Jarlais 2000). Thus the questions that Congress originally asked science to answer about needle exchange programs relative to the spread of infection and the levels of drug using (General Accounting Office 1993) have been replaced for some opponents by simple value positions that exist in a symbolic realm where scientific evidence is irrelevant. For one observer, what started as a movement based on the ideal of reducing harm among people at risk from their use of needles to inject drugs is being framed by opponents who could not find the answers they sought in science so embarked on a moral crusade based on the belief that giving needles to drug users sends the wrong message to people who already are violating the law (Moss 2000: 1386).

Theoretical foundations

When the purpose of drug policy is to allow for drugs to be available for use in personally and socially beneficial ways but not used in ways that can disrupt or damage the health and well-being of the people using them or anyone else around them (near or far), then the strategy unsurprisingly favors initiatives that support the use of drugs for therapeutic purposes, minimize any harm that people or communities might experience from inappropriate use of drugs, and employ tactics such as needle exchange, drug treatment, drug research, and education to foster responsible drug use (cf. Inciardi and Harrison 2000; Kleiman et al. 2011; Nadelmann 1992; Riley et al. 1999). The United Kingdom Harm Reduction Alliance (UKHRA) is a coalition that advocates for public health and human rights as the central concerns of drug policy emphasizing initiatives providing drug treatment and services for drug users (http://www.ukhra.org/index.html). On its website it defines this as a harm reduction drug policy in that it is oriented toward reducing the health, social, and economic harms faced by individuals, communities, and society through their association with drugs (see Newcombe 1992). Advocacy for this position in the UK is not as challenging as it would be in the US given the long history of harm reduction in the UK (Reuter and Stevens 2007). In fact, not long ago the UK Drug Policy Commission reviewed the available evidence and then released a report seeking "to consider how an explicit refocusing of drug law enforcement on the reduction of drug-related harms could deliver a real impact on the drug-related harms experienced by individuals and communities" (UK Drug Policy Commission 2009: 7).

While perhaps prematurely proclaiming in the late twentieth century that harm reduction as a drug policy was coming to the US, Marlatt identified the underlying assumptions of such a policy in the context of assumptions that support other drug policy positions. He wrote:

> Harm reduction, with its philosophical roots in pragmatism and its compatibility with a public health approach, offers a practical alternative to either the moral or disease models. Unlike proponents of the moral model, who view drug use as bad or illegal and who advocate supply reduction (via prohibition and punishment), harm reduction shifts the focus away from drug use itself to the consequences or effects of addictive behavior. Such effects are evaluated primarily in terms of whether they are harmful or helpful to the drug user and to the larger society, and not on the basis of whether the behavior itself is considered morally right or wrong. Unlike supporters of the disease model, who view addiction as a biological/genetic pathology and promote demand reduction as the primary goal of prevention and abstinence as the only acceptable goal of treatment, harm reduction offers a wide range of policies and procedures designed to reduce the harmful consequences of addictive behavior. Harm reduction accepts the practical fact that many people use drugs and engage in other high-risk behaviors and that idealistic visions of a drug-free society are unlikely to become reality.
>
> *(Marlatt 1996: 785–86)*

In that sense a harm reduction policy would assume that drug use is itself not a bad thing and that the proper focus of drug policy should be on helping people who suffer harm from their own use of drugs or the involvement with drugs of other people around them. Concern for drug use should not be about the morality of using drugs or with trying to abolish all use of drugs. It should be about responding in a caring way when drug involvement results in injurious consequences.

As in the case of a drug policy emphasizing control or regulation, ideologically it would be easy to design a harm reduction drug policy based on assumptions about drugs and drug using independent of any reputable or verifiable knowledge. A policy buttressed by theory naturally would require more substantial evidence. There would need to be valid and reliable evidence from science to demonstrate that drugs can have harmful health consequences and that addressing the harm that they may cause would be of value to society. In the late 1990s Don Des Jarlais wrote an editorial in response to the scientific evidence presented by a collection of articles on addictive substances published in an issue of the *American Journal of Public Health*. In it he wrote, "It is now abundantly clear that the nonmedical use of psychoactive drugs is one of the major causes of health problems in the United States, as reflected in the physiological effects of the drugs (overdoses and alcohol cirrhosis), behavior while under the influence of drugs (drunken driving and domestic violence), and consequences inherent in drug administration (carcinogens in tobacco smoke, human immunodeficiency virus [HIV] and other serious infections transmitted through shared injection equipment)" (Des Jarlais 1996: 10). The point is that for some time now we have known that there are harms associated with some drug use by some people in some circumstances and that there are things we can do to minimize that harm. And to the extent that our knowledge is incomplete, theory helps us to take what we know and integrate it with suitable assumptions to fill the gaps to allow us to form a logical and coherent argument in support of the policy direction being considered.

There is scientific evidence to support the belief that drugs can be viewed as a serious public health problem, and there are mainstream criminological theories starting from that point that provide policymakers with a logical and coherent argument for favoring policies that focus on reducing the health-related harms associated with drugs. The link between mainstream criminological theory and harm reduction goes back to some of the earliest thinking about criminal behavior. During the Enlightenment classical theorists took the position that humans had free will and were rational beings who would act in their own interest to maximize pleasure and minimize pain (Akers and Sellers 2008; Bernard *et al.* 2002). Notably, in 1764 Cesare Beccaria first published his classical statement on the meaning and purpose of punishment in which he argued that the only justifiable reason for punishment was deterrence (Beccaria 1963; Maestro 1973). Building on Beccaria's work, in its contemporary incarnation rational choice theory like classical theory argues that before offending a social actor makes a decision balancing the likelihood of being punished, the severity of the possible punishment, and the costs of offending against the personal requirements and the potential rewards of engaging in the offensive action (Akers and Sellers 2008; Bernard *et al.* 2002). For example, Cornish and Clarke developed a model of how an actor makes the determination to perform a criminal act suggesting that the individual seeking to benefit him or herself by the act exhibits "a measure of rationality, albeit restrained by limits of time and ability and the availability of relevant information" (Cornish and Clarke 1986: 1). In terms of harm reduction as a drug policy this theoretical perspective supports the notion that people being rational can make the choice to avoid situations that might result in personal harm, such as using drugs known to be harmful, using drugs in harmful ways, or being involved with other people who use drugs.

A challenge for rational choice theorists is that not everyone living in society acts in his or her own interest or even knows their own interest. Not everyone is aware of the possible consequences of his or her actions or even the likelihood of those consequences happening. But if we accept that people are rational beings then theoretically at least this circumstance can be remedied. The criminological learning theories of sociologists and social psychologists generally suggest that people can learn how to behave and act through interaction with others (Akers and Sellers 2008). Criminological thought was largely influenced in this regard by the work of Edwin Sutherland in his theory of differential association. He argued that criminal behavior is learned in interaction with other people, particularly through intimate personal relationships and depending on the characteristics of the association (frequency, duration, priority, and intensity), and that through this process people learn techniques, directions, and motivations for behavior (Sutherland and Cressey 1974). For Sutherland the individual learned criminal behavior through an excess of communications favorable to violations of law. Akers combined Sutherland's theory with principles of behaviorism and proposed a social learning theory arguing that learning takes place in the context of social structure, interaction, and situations so that people learn both deviant and conformist behavior and how to justify the direction they follow in their own action through reinforcement (positive and negative) and punishment (Akers 2009). In terms of the significance of social learning theory for drug policy, the point is that learning theory provides support for the belief that people can be taught to make better decisions and to act in their own interest. In fact, in his own early research on drug addiction Akers applied notions of learning theory to addiction and concluded that positive and negative reinforcement, both social and physiological, help us to understand how people become involved with or avoid particular drug use (Akers *et al.* 1968).

The issue for drug policy is whether or not harm reduction should be or should not be a more central concern. There are times and circumstances and places when people and communities do experience harm as a consequence of drug using or involvement with drugs by themselves or by other people living among them. So making policy to address that harm is not unreasonable. And mainstream criminological theories can be used to support the argument for making harm reduction the focus of drug policy. They tell us that we can and should expect people to act rationally in their own interest and that we believe we can teach people that it is rational to forsake drugs that can harm them and to use drugs when they do in ways that are defined and recognized as responsible. But if we are concerned with the harm resulting from drugs in a community then we need as well to consider the ways and extent to which drugs are or could be used in the community without resulting in any harm. We need to consider how drugs are or could be helpful to the community and the people who live there. Addressing harm is only addressing a piece of the problem. The bigger question is how to design a policy that recognizes that drugs are not always harmful and they are and always have been an important part in the lives of people living among other people in society (cf. Erickson and Hathaway 2010).

Alternative directions and questions to consider

According to a report in the *Huffington Post* on July 20, 2012, in Central and Eastern Europe the "punitive, law enforcement-focused drug policies" of the post-Soviet 1990s are starting to give way to interest in the Global Commission on Drug Policy position advocating for "evidence-based drug policies, including the decriminalization of drug use and possession of drugs for personal use, unrestricted access to treatment for people dependent on drugs, and wide provision of services that prevent drug overdose and public health crises such as HIV epidemics" (Malinowska-Sempruch 2012). For example, the article reports that in the Czech Republic the government commissioned studies and based on findings of those studies "recognized the need for ready access to health and treatment services for drug users." That is, nations in Central and Eastern Europe may be following the example of those nations in Western Europe that have adopted a drug policy to manage the harm to people and communities related to drug use and involvement rather than to control through punitive measures the behavior of those same people. But while harm reduction appears to be spreading across Europe, that is not the case in other parts of the world, particularly in non-Western nations.

Allopathic medicine is the traditional and conventional form of medicine practiced in Western nations involving medical and healthcare professionals who treat diseases and their symptoms with radiation, surgery, and drugs (WHO 2001: 1). This is not necessarily the practice in non-Western nations. In India, for example, for centuries "ayurveda, siddha, and unani systems of medicine have coexisted with yoga, naturopathy, and homeopathy," emphasizing a way of life that embraces a belief in the human body as "composed of five basic elements: earth, water, fire, air, and sky," posture and breathing exercises, meditation, contemplation, and drugless treatments (WHO 2001: 131). During the colonial period in India this traditional approach to healthcare was confronted by the allopathic medicine of the colonizers, and not always with agreeable results (WHO 2001: 132). In fact, more than a century later an inability to integrate the two persists.

According to an article in *The Times of India* on July 19, 2012, "Nearly 25,000 doctors affiliated to Ayush Federation of India's Karnataka branch will go on an indefinite strike from Friday [July 20, 2010] seeking official permission to use allopathic drugs to treat emergency cases" (http://articles. timesofindia.indiatimes.com/2012-07-19/mangalore/32746428_1_ayush-doctors-allopathic-drugs-ayush-practitioners (accessed July 21, 2012)). According to the article, under a Supreme Court ruling the state governments in India have been directed under the Drugs and Cosmetics Act, 1980 to permit medical practitioners "to prescribe allopathic drugs based on their education, training, and experience." The fact that a strike is planned suggests that the ruling has been met with opposition or at least delay. Consequently, drugs that might be able to help people are not being made available to them.

The point here is that even if the Court ruling and the legislation were to be followed and medical and healthcare practitioners in India were permitted to use drugs to treat diseases and symptoms, the issue is not one of managing harm. Beyond managing any harm from drugs to people, the issue is doing good for people with drugs. If the medical community does gain the authority to use drugs for therapeutic purposes, they would be able to help people suffering from illness and disease to get well. While there are restrictions and limits, in the Western world drug therapy already is an integral and valuable part of modern healthcare (McPhee *et al.* 2012). Also, sometimes people have found that using drugs simply gives them pleasure or relief from the mundane experience of their daily lives without causing any pain for themselves or anyone else (cf. Huxley 1954; Weil 1972). This raises an issue with the notion of harm reduction as a drug policy. Certainly there is evidence that there are personal and social harms related to the use, misuse, and abuse of certain drugs or even the use of any drugs in certain ways or in certain situations. So a policy that recognizes that problem and strives to address it is not a bad thing. But drugs also contribute to better living and better lives for people and their communities, and focusing on harms while it may not be the intention can take attention away from the positive things that drugs do or could do for users.

Theoretically, it has been shown that mainstream criminological theories including rational choice and learning theory can be used to provide support and direction for programs and initiatives favoring a harm reduction drug policy. But given an interest not only in reducing harm from drugs but also considering the positive things that drugs can contribute, critical criminological theories can suggest other directions, even when the focus is on harm reduction.

It has been argued that "To ensure a pragmatic approach to criminology with the potential to influence government, theories must be able to address the new external realities of policy making, while taking seriously postmodern critiques and remaining practical and relevant" (Wheeldon and Heidt 2007: 317). A theoretical perspective that took hold in the UK in the 1980s—left realism—arguably addresses this concern. Like other critical criminologists, left realist theorists address the "crimogenic consequences of broader social forces such as patriarchy and capitalism" (DeKeseredy 2011: 38), but also "start with the assertion that inner-city violence is a major problem for socially and economically disenfranchised people, regardless of their sex or ethnic/cultural background" (DeKeseredy 2003: 31). In that sense left realists from the beginning have distinguished their theory from both "right realism" and "left idealism" and have expressed concern for the victims of both white-collar and street-level offenders (cf. MacLean 1993; Matthews 1987; Young 1987). In that sense left realism maintains its concern for a democratic and humane appreciation for individuals and social life but recognizes the need to be practical. Harm reduction is grounded in pragmatism (Marlatt 1996) so has a logical connection to left realist criminological theory. That is, from a left realist perspective the programs and initiatives of a harm reduction policy make sense in that they view people using drugs not merely as offenders but also in terms of their own victimization.

Interestingly, while left realist criminological theory provides support for what a harm reduction drug policy does, it also points to what a harm reduction policy does not do but needs to be concerned about. In terms of public policy left realists not only consider addressing the negative things that people do or have happen to them, but also propose steps that would "enhance many people's well-being, as well as contribute to the development of strong, cohesive, and vibrant communities" (DeKeseredy 2003: 39). In terms of drug policy, that would suggest the need to be attentive not only to the harms related to drug use or drug involvement but also to the ways that drugs can be used to enhance the lives of people and their communities.

The purpose of this chapter is not to argue that harm reduction is a bad drug policy. In fact, compared to a control or regulatory drug policy, which are oriented to public safety, a harm reduction policy that is oriented to public health adds important ideas and initiatives and notably introduces the notion that drug policy needs to be just and humane and to care about the health and well-being of people and their communities. Still, to the extent that a drug policy would be based on or even include harm reduction there are questions that need to be addressed. For example: What health problems do people experience from using different drugs in different circumstances, and what can we do to minimize the negative consequences? How do we determine which drugs are harmful and when they are harmful, and which drugs are beneficial and when? When, how, and why should we try to prevent people from using drugs, as opposed to when, how, and why we might allow or even encourage drug use? When, how, and why might we encourage anyone to enter drug treatment? Do efforts to address harm in any way or ever create problems in that drugs that can help people become unavailable? Does focusing on harm put more emphasis on the negative things drugs can do and take away attention to the positive things? The determination of the appropriate place for harm reduction in a drug policy would benefit from further debate on questions such as these.

4

THE DEBATE OVER VALUE

Perhaps the person with the single greatest influence on drug policy in the US during the twentieth century was Harry Jacob Anslinger. Officially, he served as Commissioner of the US Treasury Department's Federal Bureau of Narcotics (FBN) from its formation in 1930 until 1962, when he became the US Representative to the United Nations Narcotics Commission. His status as a government agent gave him the responsibility and authority to initiate and advance national policy on drug use and distribution. More important, it gave him a platform to advocate for his own beliefs, opinions, and values about drugs and the people who use them. Ultimately, he was able to set a foundation for a national drug policy agenda that would assign a negative value to drug users and to drugs, drug use, and drug distribution as invariably and inevitably harmful to people and destructive to their communities.

Anslinger focused a good part of his attention on marijuana. In 1937, just before the federal government introduced legislation to assert control over marijuana use and distribution, in *The American Magazine* he wrote, "How many murders, suicides, robberies, criminal assaults, hold-ups, burglaries, and deeds of maniacal insanity [marijuana] causes each year, especially among the young, can only be conjectured" (Anslinger and Cooper 1937; cited in Kaplan 1971: 92). It was a fair statement. At the time there were lots of stories in newspapers making claims but there was no statistical or scientific evidence so he had no way of knowing the answer. Despite the lack of evidence available to answer his question, throughout the decade he nonetheless wrote a number of articles about marijuana. By himself or with co-authors he wrote articles with names like "Marijuana, Assassin of Youth," "Youth Gone Loco," and "One More Peril for Youth" (Inciardi 2007; McWilliams 1990; Sloman 1979).

Since he could not cite nonexistent scientific or statistical evidence, in his own writings Anslinger told unsubstantiated stories about the evils of marijuana and marijuana users. For example, in his article in *The American Magazine* he wrote the following:

> During the last year a young male addict was hanged in Baltimore for criminal assault on a ten-year-old girl. His defense was that he was temporarily insane from smoking marijuana. In Alamosa, Colo., a degenerate brutally attacked a young girl while under the influence of the drug. In Chicago, two marijuana smoking boys murdered a policeman.
>
> *(Anslinger and Cooper 1937)*

The article provided no evidence that any of these stories represent an event that actually links marijuana use and the criminal or violent behavior being associated with it, or even that these events actually ever occurred. Still Anslinger did not hesitate to vilify marijuana and its users as evil. He opened the article with the following:

> The sprawled body of a young girl lay crushed on the sidewalk the other day after a plunge from the fifth story of a Chicago apartment house. Everyone called it suicide, but actually it was murder. The killer was a narcotic known to America as marijuana, and to history as hashish. It is a narcotic used in the form of cigarettes, comparatively new to the United States and as dangerous as a coiled rattlesnake.
>
> *(Anslinger and Cooper 1937)*

Thus with disregard for evidence of authenticity or even reasonableness Harry Anslinger set the stage for an assault on drugs, drug users, and drug distributors blatantly based on beliefs, opinions, and values rather than reason, science, and knowledge.

There were questions being asked about the validity of his claims, so Anslinger used his position with the US Treasury Department to give his beliefs and values credence in the absence of evidence. On January 14, 1937 Commissioner Anslinger bolstered his argument at a formal conference called by the Treasury Department. Growing impatient with the few lawyers and scientists at the event talking about what little they or anyone knew about marijuana he asked: "What are the proofs that the use of marijuana, in any of its forms, is habit-forming or addictive, and what are the indications and positive proofs that such addiction develops socially undesirable characteristics in the user?" (Sloman 1979: 57). Then he went on to answer his own question presenting the same uncorroborated and often specious stories he had been telling in his published articles, stories that famously came to be known as his "gore file" (Sloman 1979: 57). There was the story about a marijuana smoking man in Baltimore who killed a 10-year-old girl, and the violence in Colorado caused by degenerates who became insane after using marijuana. And there were others:

West Va.—Negro raped a girl of eight years of age. Two Negroes took a girl fourteen years old and kept her for two days in a hut under the influence of marijuana. Upon recovery she was found to be suffering from syphilis.

In New Jersey in 1936, a particularly brutal murder occurred, in which case one young man killed another, literally smashing his face and head to a pulp. One of the defenses was that the defendant's intellect was so prostrated from his smoking Marihuana cigarettes that he did not know what he was doing. ... The fury of the murder was apparent. Not content with killing his friend, he tore out his tongue, his eyes, and so mutilated him that even the hardened coroner had to turn his eyes away from the gruesome sight.

Anslinger ended his presentation by telling those present that while he was certain about the evils of marijuana neither he nor the Treasury Department could be responsible for the accuracy of the information he provided and that he lacked any more details about the events he described (Sloman 1979: 57).

Later in 1937 Anslinger took his disapproving beliefs and values about drugs to Congress in support of the Marijuana Tax Act, a revenue bill intended to collect taxes from people engaged in marijuana transactions but also designed for the federal government to assert control over marijuana and its users and distributors (Inciardi 2007; Musto 1999; Smith 1988). Hearings were held before the Committee on Ways and Means of the House of Representatives during the First Session of the Seventy-Fifth Congress on April 27, 28, 29, 30, and May 4, 1937 on bill number HR 6385, *Taxation of Marihuana*. The Commissioner of the Federal Bureau of Narcotics, Harry Anslinger, was first to testify. As expected, he presented the Committee stories from his gore file (see page 22 in the record of his testimony before Congress):

MR. ANSLINGER: I will give you gentlemen just a few outstanding evidences of crimes that have been committed as a result of the use of marihuana.

MR. [DANIEL A.] REED [REP. FROM NEW YORK]: The testimony before the committee of which I was formerly chairman in reference to heroin said in reference to the effect of it that it made men feel fearless, and that a great majority of the crimes of great violence that were committed were committed by addicts, and one man stated that it would make a rabbit fight a bulldog. Does this drug [marihuana] have a similar effect?

MR. ANSLINGER: Here is a gang of seven young men, all seven of them, young men under 21 years of age. They terrorized central Ohio for more than two months, and they were responsible for 38 stick-ups. They all boast they did these crimes while under the influence of marihuana.

MR. [DAVID J.] LEWIS [REP. FROM MARYLAND]: Was that an excuse, or a defense?

MR. ANSLINGER: No, sir.

MR. LEWIS: Does it strengthen the criminal will; does it operate as whisky might, to provoke recklessness?

MR. ANSLINGER: I think it makes them irresponsible. A man does not know what he is doing. It has not been recognized as a defense by the courts, although it has been used as a defense.

MR. LEWIS: Probably the word "excuse" or "mitigation" would be better than defense, I think.

MR. ANSLINGER: Here is one of the worst cases I have seen. The district attorney told me the defendant in this case pleaded that he was under the influence of marihuana when he committed that crime, but that has not been recognized. We have several cases of that kind. There was one town in Ohio where a young man went into a hotel and held up the clerk and killed him, and his defense was that he had been affected by the use of marihuana.

Thus as usual, Anslinger told stories he had read or heard and was not prepared to provide any actual evidence in support of anything he said. So four years after the repeal of the Constitutional Amendment prohibiting the use of alcohol, the US Congress passed the Marijuana Tax Act.

Anslinger's legacy endures (Meisler 1996) and for generations to follow drug policy in the US has been based at least as much on beliefs and values as on reason or knowledge. A few years before Anslinger died in 1975, John Kaplan wrote, "In weighing the evidence on the connection between marijuana and aggression, one is struck by two things: one is the relatively large number of statements made by policy-making committees, medical societies, and public officials as compared with the relatively small number of studies that actually bear on this issue; the other is the even more striking fact that the studies and evidence relied on in these statements are of extremely weak probative value" (Kaplan 1971: 92). Ultimately, the problem is that this situation has eliminated the possibility of having any open and honest discourse or public debate on the value and values of drugs and the people involved with them, negative or positive. This should not be the case in a free and democratic society, but the Anslinger example regarding drug policy suggests that at least in the case of drugs it has been.

Social, cultural, and historical context

According to his biographical statement on the website of the Criminal Justice Policy Foundation (CJPF), Eric Sterling has been advocating for drug policy reform at least since he became President of the Foundation in 1989 (http://www.cjpf.org/about/biography). Prior to joining the CJPF, from 1979 to 1989 he served as Counsel to the US House of Representatives Committee on the Judiciary and staff to the

Subcommittee on Crime, where his responsibilities included among other things drug enforcement policy and legislation. He played a significant role in the development of the Comprehensive Crime Control Act of 1984 and the Anti-Drug Abuse Acts of 1986 and 1988. After decades of thinking about and contributing to drug policy in the US, Sterling wrote an article in which he argued "that the war on drugs is based on retributive values that are illogical, burden the criminal justice system, and are ineffective in reducing drug-related harm" (Sterling 2004: 51). He went on to say that "segregation was a form of nonjudicial punishment for blacks until 1970, and ... the war on drugs has become a punishment substitute for segregation" (Sterling 2004: 51). That is, according to a long time analyst and observer of drug policy in the US, contemporary drug policy not only is grounded in punitive values but also explicitly serves as a means through which the position and worth of certain members of society are diminished relative to others by linking them to something deemed morally reprehensible, in this case drugs (or at least particular drugs, or drugs used in particular ways).

Others have similarly observed that drug policy in the US since the early twentieth century has been built on a foundation of values and beliefs rather than knowledge or reason. For example, earlier we noted how prominent drug historians and social scientists like David Musto (1999), Troy Duster (1970), James Inciardi (2007), and others in one way or another concluded that American drug policy has viewed and continues to view drug users as weak, drug dealers as evil, and drugs themselves as invariably harmful, though not all drugs and not all people and not all the time. That is, the policy over time has been selective favoring some people over others and opposing some drugs and not others. In itself that is not necessarily problematic. It becomes a problem when the values represented are those of a select group and there is no opportunity for open debate or discourse in which all values and their impact on all people can be considered. That is why it is important that in the case of drug policy a full and satisfactory open debate about values has not taken place.

From the beginning the media have played a role in supporting the negative value placed on drugs, drug users, and drug distributors. In 1936, a year before Harry Anslinger presented tales from his gore file to the Congressional Committee, a film called *Reefer Madness* was released in movie theaters around the US. Following an onscreen notice that "incidents and characters portrayed in this motion picture are purely fictional," the film opened with a rolling script telling viewers that the film was based on "actual research" and that what they were about to see could happen to their own children. The script warned that while "events may startle you" it had to be that way since the filmmakers needed to " ... sufficiently emphasize the frightful toll of the new drug menace which is destroying the youth of America in alarmingly increasing numbers. *Marijuana* is the drug—a violent narcotic—an unspeakable scourge—the *Real Public Enemy Number One!*" In the film itself a group of clean cut high school students are seduced by slightly older men with unkempt hair and maniacal stares into using marijuana. Naturally, they all start acting out in strange ways and a young girl is murdered. At no time is there any further reference to the "actual research."

Over the years there have been countless examples of news stories, films, books, and now blogs and other high speed cyber forms of communication that in a variety of ways place value on drugs and the people involved with them. This is not to say that there are not also media messages more supportive of drugs and drug users, but particularly in the contemporary words of people hidden behind the anonymity of their screen names and the obscurity of cyberspace we can see the wanton meanness that people bring through media to *other people* who are involved with drugs *other than the ones they themselves use*. For example, Yahoo!, a major web search engine, has a page where it invites people to submit questions to which others can respond (http://answers.yahoo.com/info/about;_ylt=AvtfGMXPYt.z506RLRF19LHj1KIX;_ylv=3). At Yahoo! Answers when you post your question you are given guidelines about being courteous and not mean. Here are some questions posted over the past few years:

Addiction is for the weak willed and weak minded, true or false?
Do You Agree That Drug Users are Weak Minded?
Who else agrees drug users are weak minded and inferior?
What are your perceptions on drug addicts if you are NOT one?

One reader responded to the last question by saying, "I think that drug addicts are morons because if you hadn't done drugs in the first place you wouldn't be addicted." Obviously, these are not representative of anything and mixed into the comments are statements that are sympathetic to drug users as well as those that are demeaning. But the point is that these sentiments are put out there into the public arena by people who feel free to speak their mind without concern that anyone will know who they are.

Traditional media like newspapers and magazines have bylines by the people writing stories, but not the people who submit comments via the online editions. Interestingly, given the anonymity of the people submitting comments, these news articles and the attached comments may be the closest we can get to an open discourse about our values concerning drugs, drug users, and drug distributors. For example, on January 13, 2012 the *New York Post* ran a story called *120 from LI arrested on drug charges stemming from "Heroin Highway"*. Under the byline "Associated Press" the story told how 120 middle class men and women between the ages 20 and 25 living in suburban communities in Queens and on Long Island were arrested and charged as heroin dealers. The story itself was mostly descriptive but was interesting because the alleged dealers and customers were middle class and suburban and the drug was heroin. This made for interesting comments, including the following [sic]:

So my tax dollars is now going to be used to rehabilitate drug snorting and shooting losers? That sucks. ... I say bring thailands law on durgs on any one who snorts it or deals it gets life in prison or gets to meet his maker. That would deter most of these losers.

I wonder why all of a sudden we are worrying about how these junkies got started? I bet your comments would be a lot different if this story was about a bust in Harlem instead of Suffolk County where most of the people were arrested. I guess because the junkies and drug dealers came from "good families".

Well, well, well, hummmmmmmmmmmmm so all these drug bust on Eastern Long Island, you could hear all that wrist slapping all the way to Manhattan! Who cares, all this shows is that drug abuse and addiction see's no color, hopefully they and many others can rise above the madness and move on with better cleaner lives.

No names of suspects, in Yawn Island, must be plenty of white people involved ...

These are not all the comments, but they show what at least some of the people writing comments think of drug users, and also reflects opinions about the significance of race when it comes to drugs and related values.

Across the country in California an article appeared in the *Los Angeles Times* on November 7, 2011 called "White and mixed-race youths rank high in alcohol, substance abuse" written by Melissa Healy of the *Times*. Like the New York story it was mostly descriptive. It reported on survey results showing that mixed race youth have a similar pattern of drug abuse to white adolescents, which the article found troubling given the high rate of substance abuse disorders among white adolescents. The reader comments, however, were more interested in the race of the users than the problems faced by the kids. For example [sic]:

- When I drive thru Watts, Inglewood & S Central LA for business, & see usually dozens of young, black males drinking on sidewalks, in alleys & on vacant lots, pushing shopping carts & talking to themselves, they must be downing Dr Pepper. Brown paper bagging it, before noon on weekdays. Never seen anything close to that in Koreatown or Redondo Beach. Who to believe, the PC LA Times or my lying eyes …
- Blacks are just a notch or two above Asians? I'm sure that all those purveyors of the stereotype of Blacks as prolific substance abusers compared to Whites will take note of this and change their rhetoric accordingly.
- "'the child took hazardous risks under the influence' Like drove home, which is more common in the lower-density suburbs & rural areas than inner-cities. (alcohol, marijuana, cocaine, inhalants, hallucinogens, heroin, analgesic opioids, stimulants, sedatives, and tranquilizers)" Of course, since hallucinogens & mom's anti-depressant's are more commonly available in white areas, those drugs will appear on surveys more than in inner-cities with different intoxicants of choice. & that survey link doesn't show basic data like questions asked & population details. Typical. Keep spinning hard left, LA Times.

Again, this is not representative and not inclusive, but it does show there are some very negative and race-based feelings out there about drug users.

And it does show how low the level of dialogue can go about how we feel about drug users.

Every year since 1988 on June 26 people in nations across the world celebrate the United Nations International Day Against Drug Abuse and Illicit Trafficking. Individuals, organizations, and communities participate in events to raise awareness of what is considered the major problem of illicit drugs in society through an expression of "determination to strengthen action and cooperation to achieve the goal of an international society free of drug abuse" (http://www.un.org/en/events/drugabuseday/). In 2012 the theme of the day was Global Action for Healthy Communities without Drugs. In Oman the Health Ministry held a ceremony and showed a documentary "advising youth on how to protect themselves from drugs" and including "an exhibition on drugs and their dire consequences" (*Oman Daily Observer*, July 2, 2012). The day was also celebrated in the Indian state of Kerala where the Minister for Excise told the media that "it is shameful and disappointing that the State still ranks high in liquor consumption" and that if children can be directed away from using such substances it will "improve family relations which, in turn, will lead to an overall betterment of the society" (*The Hindu*, June 27, 2012). In the Bahamas the day was celebrated with a focus on youth to make sure they got the message that, "It is a well-proven fact that drugs are dangerous. The euphoric or pleasurable effects experienced are short-lived, while the adverse effects are far-reaching and have a devastating impact on one's psychological, physiological, social and spiritual well-being" (http://thebahamasweekly.com, June 21, 2012). Overall the day was an opportunity to spread the word that drugs are a problem. In a Google news search I could not find any reference to any day that celebrates drugs that save lives or ease the living of people who are suffering. There may be one, but I could not find it.

Theoretical foundation

It is hard to imagine that any government in any free and democratic nation would openly and deliberately advance a policy that calls for the devaluation of any of its citizens. But that does not mean that there are no policies that do just that, though in such cases it is not surprising when the intention of the policy is oblique or even concealed. When the intended purpose of a drug policy is to devalue people because they use drugs or to devalue people or communities because their drug of choice or their method of using or obtaining drugs is not legally authorized or recognized as socially acceptable, then the strategy would emphasize marginalization or disenfranchisement using socially constructed categories of difference to justify divisive tactics like restrictive employment and housing practices or disciplinary tactics like arrest and imprisonment allowing for the separation of some people but not others from access to societal resources (cf. Brownstein 2000; Duster 1970; Husch 1992; Lynch 2012; Provine 2011; Welch *et al.* 1998). There are organizations established for a variety of purposes that assert broadly that being involved with drugs is a bad thing. For example, on LIVESTRONG.COM, a website associated with the Lance Armstrong Foundation for helping people who want to "build their own healthy living success story," there recently was an article called "Bad effects of drug abuse" arguing that "While drug use can induce feelings of euphoria and high sensations in someone, the negative consequences generally outweigh these feelings. Drug abuse negatively affects all aspects of people's lives and even though they are aware of these bad effects, their desire to use the drug overpowers their desire for positive relationships and success in work or school" (Butler 2010). While the Lance Armstrong website assigns negative value to drugs and drug users, that value is placed in a context of good health. In a religious context the assignment of negative value on drugs and drug users is more direct. For example, OpenBible.info, a website focusing on religion, has a page called Bible Verses about Drug Addiction. This page provides a list of Bible verses about the evil of drugs and drug use and an opportunity for readers to add their own verses to the list (http://www.openbible.info/topics/drug_addiction). For example, Peter 5:8 offers a general warning statement: "Be sober-minded; be watchful. Your adversary the devil prowls around like a roaring lion, seeking someone to devour." In case the reference to drugs as the devil is not clear enough, more directly referring to a drug of choice during the time of the Bible is Proverbs 20:1: "Wine is a mocker, a strong drink a brawler, and whoever is led astray by it is not wise." Or there is Ephesians 5:18: "And do not get drunk with wine, for that is debauchery, but be filled with the Spirit." Statements like these can be used to give moral authority to the devaluation of drugs and drug users and can be used to justify their subsequent separation from society and social life.

The point here is not whether claims about the badness of people involved with drugs are based in reality or whether the people or organizations making such claims are representative of a broad segment of society. The point is that such claims do exist, there are people and organizations that make them, and those people and organizations have easily found ideological support for their claims. In the absence of empirical evidence to support their claims they turn to religious aphorisms and the like to ground those claims in a cloak of moral certainty and righteousness. Ideologically, they can make ethical assumptions about the worth of other people and the morality of their behavior and epistemological assumptions about the veracity of their own claims.

An interesting thing about the debate on value in regard to drug policy is that compared to either the debate on controlling behavior or the debate on managing harm, it rests more heavily on assumptions. The questions it raises are about value, so the measures and methods of science inherently are less useful for addressing them. For example, whether all or any people by nature are good or bad does not readily lend itself to observation and measurement. Whether a person who uses drugs is worth less than a person who does not is a matter of opinion. Whether it is fair to give less of societal resources to people who are involved with particular drugs defined as illegal and more to people who instead use other drugs that are defined as legal is not a testable question. As a result it is almost necessary to ground a drug policy based on values in ideology. Theory is part of the scientific process of building evidence and advancing knowledge, so the policymaker making drug policy based on values has more limited use for theory.

In summary, it is difficult to justify with reason and knowledge a drug policy based on values. There is less empirical evidence and more assumption. There is a surfeit of opinion and judgment concerning other people and the things they do. So different from control-based or management-based drug policy, it is not easy to find societies that openly implement a value-based drug policy. But there is evidence that value-based initiatives are at least part of broader drug policies as seen in things like the arrest and incarceration rates of even minor drug users in certain societies and the employment and housing restrictions on drug users in certain communities. And there are mainstream criminological theories that provide a theoretical foundation to hide behind for these policies or initiatives within policies.

A policy based on the valuation or devaluation of people, behavior, or artifacts needs to be able to make explicit distinctions within each of these categories and to be able to assign subjective meaning to those distinctions. For example, it would be necessary to distinguish one type of person from another and to be able to argue that the avowed difference between them would result in different consequences or outcomes. In criminology this kind of thinking goes back to the nineteenth century theories of the biological positivists (Bernard *et al.* 2002) like Lombroso, who distinguished the physical characteristics of prisoners from soldiers (Lombroso-Ferrero and Savitz 1972). In the decades since there has been ongoing research trying to find a connection between biological or physical characteristics and criminal behavior, with attention most recently focusing on the brain (Denno 1988; Fishbein 1990; Wilson and Herrnstein 1985; Koob and Volkow 2010).

In terms of drugs, a drug may be categorized as "any biologic agent that affects biologic function" and while not all drugs are addictive when they are then the resulting addiction "in many ways is like infectious diseases" infecting some people but not others (Goldstein 2001: 4, 12). So even more than criminal behavior, it would be possible to argue that different patterns and problems of drug use could be linked to biological or physical differences in different ways. Based on years of clinical experience and research, Avram Goldstein in his book on addiction wrote that while addictive drugs have serious health consequences for users and can pose a threat to nonusers as well, "addiction has multiple causes, many preventive strategies, and many approaches to treatment" (Goldstein 2001: 5). He went on to conclude that even in the case of addiction, let alone behavior, while biological and in particular genetic factors need to be considered so do environmental influences and social patterns (Goldstein 2001: 103). Thus simple solutions, such as separating drug users from nonusers, will not adequately address the problem. In fact, Goldstein emphasizes the need for a solid foundation of scientific knowledge to buttress our theories and guide our policies on drugs when he writes in the Preface to the second edition of his book, "This book is about the science of drug addiction—how we know what we know, what we still need to learn, and how what we learn must inform rational policies. Reader, you will find no ideology here and no sermons about morality, but only honest evaluations of the present state of addiction science by an addiction scientist" (Goldstein 2001: xii).

Goldstein's work does provide support for the notion of a relationship between human biology and drug using. It does not however offer a basis to distinguish the worth of people who use drugs relative to others who do not. Rather it suggests that while there are people who cannot quit using drugs once they start, that is not true for most people who ever use drugs, even drugs known to be addictive. He wrote:

> Of all the people who try an addictive drug, some will never use it again; they just don't like it. Some are willing to use it occasionally, to enjoy it socially with friends; but it is not important to them and they can happily do without it. Some become regular users and integrate the drug into their lives, but nevertheless are able to give it up without much trouble if they decide to. Finally, there are those who use a drug frequently and regularly and find themselves unable to quit, or at least can quit only with the greatest difficulty, and even then are likely to relapse. This last group—the addicts— represents the greatest problem for society and the greatest challenge for medical science.
>
> *(Goldstein 2001: 99)*

Those people who become addicts may become a problem for medicine and for society, but even in their case the evidence does not show that their addiction is related to being a bad person or behaving badly. It cannot. The valuation of a person or behavior is a subjective determination.

Labeling theory is a mainstream criminological theory that could be used to support an argument that people or their behavior or even artifacts are in fact good or bad. For labeling theorists the characteristics or behavior of individuals or the things in their lives are not as important for social experience as are the labels attached to them by others or even by themselves (Becker 1963; Lemert 1967). The notion is based on the earlier work of social theorists who explored the symbolic nature of meaning in relation to interpersonal communication and social interaction (Blumer 1969; Cooley 1922; Mead 1934). Labeling theorists made the argument that what they were explaining was how more powerful people and institutions are able to stigmatize and effectively devalue others and thereby diminish their experience of society. It was not intended to be used to justify stigmatization or devaluation of people or their behavior. Nonetheless, it helps explain how it is possible for drugs, drug users, and illicit drug distributors to be stigmatized so that people involved with prohibited drugs or unsanctioned ways of using authorized drugs become outsiders with more limited access to the resources and rewards of society.

Alternative directions and questions to consider

William Raspberry died on July 17, 2012 at the age of 76. For 40 years until his retirement in 2005 he had been a columnist for the *Washington Post*. In 1994 he won a Pulitzer Prize, only the second African American columnist to win the award for Commentary. On April 8, 1968, just days after Martin Luther King, Jr was assassinated, Raspberry wrote a column for the *Post* titled "Nation now must commit itself to King's principles" (http://www.washingtonpost.com/opinions/nation-now-must-commit-itself-to-kings-principles/2012/07/17/gJQAJ1OfrW_story.html (accessed July 18, 2012)). In it he suggested that while by a life cut short we would never know for certain the goals of Dr King's crusade, we do know that King was committed to a massive movement to undo what racial discrimination has done to black Americans. In much of his writing Raspberry has argued that black people themselves need to seize the opportunity at every open door, but in light of the riots that followed the King assassination in this column he wrote, "Society cannot spend centuries teaching people that they are worthless and then be surprised when they show signs of believing it." In the decades since there have been new opportunities for black Americans, but also new and innovative forms of prejudice and discrimination. Given things in the US like the disproportionate number of black people arrested and incarcerated for minor drug offenses and the selection of drugs or forms of drugs used by black people as favored targets of law and law enforcement, it is easily possible to argue that drugs have become an innovative though more subtle way to stigmatize, devalue, and thus discriminate against black Americans.

As noted earlier, a value-based drug policy is hard to justify given that the empirical evidence needed to support the conclusion that one type of person or object should be valued higher or lower than another is not logically obtainable. Therefore any such policy would need to be built on assumptions that are based on beliefs, attitudes, and opinions concerning other people who are not us, in particular what they are like and the things they do. Consequently, while there are many nations that have drug policies with control and regulation or harm reduction as their intended purpose, there are not a lot of free and democratic nations that explicitly and openly declare and promote a value-based drug policy. Nonetheless, there is evidence that such policies exist, as observed in the things that national and local governments do, such as their selection of particular groups of people to arrest and incarcerate for even minor drug offenses, the distribution of healthcare related to drugs for some people more than for others (both through the provision of expensive and health-promoting drugs when they are needed and the provision of treatment for the misuse or abuse of drugs when they become a problem), the distinction between when drug using for pleasure can be considered recreational (e.g. alcohol) and when it cannot (e.g. marijuana), and the employment and housing restrictions in certain neighborhoods and communities faced by certain categories of people who are users of certain kinds of drugs. So arguably there are drug policies that are based on values rather than evidence, even though particular strategies or initiatives might be concealed in the context of another type of drug policy and therefore are hard to notice, unless you are one of those people being devalued by the policy.

Still, there are critical criminological theories that as theories are built on ideas that point to relevant questions that can be asked and addressed by scientific research. That is, it is possible to find direction for study and learning that could inform policy even if the basis of the policy is the evaluation of the worth of people and objects. Actually, since theory is intended to be part of the scientific process of building knowledge from empirical evidence, there is no way any theory could help to answer questions about subjectively assigned values. Rather, in this case these theoretical perspectives would be helpful in exposing the flaws and limitations of a value-based drug policy.

Inevitably, when we use critical criminological theory to raise and address questions about drug policy in terms of social values, we get into discussions of power, race, gender, and other social characteristics. In this case then we can actually begin by looking at a mainstream criminological theory—labeling—which arguably has been considered by some to be a critical theoretical perspective in that it reminds criminologists that they need to consider the significance of power and social characteristics in the labeling or stigmatization of certain people and not others as criminal (Bohm and Vogel 2011). That begins to raise questions broadly for us about making drug policy dependent on values and valuation, but more directly relevant to the challenge of making meaningful, productive, and effective drug policy is what we can learn from cultural criminological theory about the role of social institutions in the social production of crime and criminals (Ferrell 2003; Ferrell and Sanders 1995). Cultural criminologists have focused on "the role of image, style, symbolic meaning among criminals and their subcultures, in the mass media's representation of crime and criminal justice, and in public conflicts over crime and crime control" (Ferrell 2003: 71). In that sense it raises questions about how individuals—who they are, and what they do or do not do—have meaning and value assigned to them by those social institutions with the power to impose that meaning and value, including not only media but also government at various levels and even things like family, language, and education. In terms of drug policy it opens the opportunity to think about and explore how and why certain drugs, certain categories of drug users, and certain forms of drug use and involvement become portrayed in the public domain as having less social value.

The theoretical thinking of left realist criminologists provides another perspective that can be useful for directing our thinking and research about the way drug policy may be used to value and devalue individuals, social activity and behavior, and societal artifacts. Martin Schwartz wrote simply that the basic premise of left realism is that "we must take crime seriously" (Schwartz 1989: 1). We have ample evidence that some drugs in some circumstances result in personal or social harms or both. So from a left realist perspective we need to take drugs seriously and be responsive. Ideally, this could even be possible through some variations of a thoughtful and fair-minded control or harm-reduction policy. But at the same time left realists recognize that while criminal justice agencies and agents need to be cognizant of and responsive to the problems related to drug use and involvement for people and communities, what they do should "not be simply re-tooled versions of the punitive, control-oriented strategies of the right" (Michalowski 1990: 2). In terms of drug policy as it relates to the valuation and devaluation of social phenomena (including people), this would be good news except under the control of powerful social institutions, drug policy through the enforcement and application of law tends to be selective. Research and history have shown, "Whatever the claims of those who write and enforce drug laws and policies, minorities and the poor are the focus of their efforts" (Brownstein 1991b: 2). That is, from left realist criminological theory we are given a perspective of drug policy that encourages us to recognize, acknowledge, and address real problems associated with drug use and involvement, but at the same time demands of us that we recognize and acknowledge that we cannot depend on old ways that devalued and stigmatized certain drugs, certain people who use drugs, and certain ways of using drugs and instead need to be innovative and find new ways to address problems while showing respect for people and their communities.

The purpose of this chapter is to highlight a focal concern of drug policy that cannot be justified in a civil society and therefore has not been openly declared by any sanctioned agency or agent of any free and open society as a formal drug policy. However, value-based elements exist through the application and practice of many established drug policies. In established drug policies that are oriented in other ways, such as control or harm reduction, researchers have observed there to be legislation, programs, and practices that make distinctions that value and devalue drugs generally and specific drugs in particular, some people who use certain drugs though not other people who use other drugs, certain settings for and ways of using drugs or being involved with drugs and not others, and even the reasons people do or do not use any drugs or particular drugs. So we need to include in our public discourse and debate about drug policy questions about values, even if it would not always be possible to obtain empirical evidence from scientific study to address them. For example: Do particular drugs or drugs generally have value? Is there a legitimate place for drugs in society? Must drugs have any assigned value, and if so who and what should determine their value? If they need to have value, must it be social or can it be personal? Must it be therapeutic or is recreation a worthy value? Is it reasonable for people to use drugs just for pleasure, and if they do is it unreasonable to avoid judging them for it? Broadly, this debate would ask the question of whether or not and if so when particular drugs should be deemed worthy of being accessible for use by some or all people, for what purposes, and under what circumstances. Given the hidden nature of values and valuation in drug policies with other stated goals, this discourse and debate may be least likely to take place, but is perhaps the one most needed.

5
CASE STUDIES

The unintended consequences of ill-informed policies

Sometime in the middle of the 1980s crack cocaine found its way onto city streets in the US. Before that there had been powder cocaine and some freebase cocaine, but not crack cocaine. From a strictly business perspective crack made a lot of sense. At the time the illicit drug market in the US was experiencing an oversupply of high quality cocaine (Office of National Drug Control Policy 1989; Office of the Attorney General 1989). Powder cocaine was expensive and while popular among wealthier white drug users, poorer black drug users could not afford it. But there was known to be an established demand for illicit drugs among urban poor people. So the business problem was how to market the abundance of cocaine in a way that would be economical enough for poor people to buy it. Crack was the answer (Bourgois 1995; Brownstein 1996; Williams 1992; Witkin 1991). It was packaged to sell so that users could buy a single hit for a small amount of money, what students of drug markets called a "marketing innovation" (Reinarman and Levine 1997). And from the business perspective it had the added advantage that the high was very intense and only lasted a very short time followed by a powerful desire for more (Inciardi et al. 1993; Johnson et al. 1992). For the seller this meant lots of repeat sales and greater profits while for the buyer what seemed like a bargain really was not. A buyer might start out thinking a few dollars would get him or her high, but before his or her run was over they would need so many hits to stay high that the cost typically would exceed their available assets. This all made for a bit of tension between buyers and sellers.

New York City was one of the first US cities where crack had established itself and was drawing a lot of attention from the local media (Brownstein 1991a). The New York *Daily News* reported on December 30, 1988 on the growing homicide rate in one section of the city and declared, "Crack whips killing toll." On May 28, 1989 there was an editorial in *The New York Times* telling readers that crack cocaine "destroy[s] the quality of life, and life itself." While the media apparently had all the answers, for social scientists interested in drugs and violence there were more questions than there were answers. But for policymakers there were decisions to be made and actions to be taken so answers were needed and correct or not they were needed fast.

At the time I was working for the New York State government in an office that was created specifically to provide state policymakers with evidence from statistics and research to support policy decisions and actions. Given the interests of the state government policymakers and my interest as a sociologist in drugs and violence, I entered into collaboration with researchers in private research organization in New York City, then called Narcotic and Drug Research, Inc. (NDRI). From that point forward I have been engaged in the study of drugs and drug markets with special attention to the relationship between research and policy.

During the 1980s and 1990s my attention was mostly on crack cocaine markets and later it shifted to methamphetamine markets. From a sociological perspective both were and are interesting in terms of how they are organized, how they operate, and how they relate to the lives of the people who participate in them and the people who share experience with those people. But both are also interesting because despite limited knowledge about how they are organized, how they operate, and their impact on people and communities, policymakers desperate to respond made decisions and took actions that were at least as strongly grounded in beliefs and values based on ideology as they were grounded in knowledge based on scientific evidence. For a social scientist interested in the relationship between research and policy, both proved to be particularly interesting because the policies that were introduced to address them resulted in unintended consequences that arguably made things worse rather than better.

In this chapter the stories are told of the unintended consequences of policies designed and implemented to address the problems of crack cocaine and crack markets and methamphetamine and meth markets. The story of crack markets is about a policy to control the markets by enforcing laws against the people participating in the market. The story of meth markets is about a policy to control the markets by making it more difficult to obtain the raw materials needed to make meth. These stories both demonstrate what happens when policies or programs are designed and implemented without scientific evidence of what they might or might not accomplish, and what might happen even if it was not intended. Policies and programs that are not thought through and are based on unproven or at best limited evidence and illogical or inadequate theories, or worse still ideology, inevitably have consequences that could not have been anticipated or intended. And sometimes, as in the case of crack cocaine and methamphetamine policies, may result in consequences that are not only unintended but also undesirable.

Crack cocaine

Harry Anslinger may have led the charge to make drugs the enemy in the US, but it was not until Richard Nixon was President in 1971 that war was formally declared. Even then the war on drugs did not really begin until the US Congress passed the Anti-Drug Abuse Act of 1988 and then President George Bush (the first) created the Office of National Drug Control Policy (ONDCP). That year the drug that most captured public attention was crack cocaine, and the first director of ONDCP, the so-called "drug czar," William Bennett, made crack his primary target. In his first *National Drug Control Strategy* in 1989 he wrote, "Crack is responsible for the fact that vast patches of the American urban landscape are rapidly deteriorating beyond effective control by civil authorities. Crack is responsible for the explosion in recent drug-related emergencies—a 28-fold increase in hospital admissions involving cocaine smoked since 1984. Crack use is increasingly responsible for the continued marketing success enjoyed by a huge international cocaine trafficking industry, with all its consequential evils. And crack is spreading—like a plague"

(ONDCP 1989: 3). The message was clear and certain despite the fact that crack cocaine had only been around for a few years and the research that could support these claims had yet to be conducted.

Crack cocaine was first observed in New York City around 1985. According to official crime statistics in the US reported by the Federal Bureau of Investigation (FBI) in its Uniform Crime Reports (UCR), the homicide rate in New York City increased by 60 per cent from 1985 to 1990. A simple explanation was that crack was to blame. Research on crack and violence conducted in the city at the time showed that there was a connection between crack and homicide, but the observed relationship was with the crack markets rather than the ingestion of the drug (Brownstein 1996; Goldstein *et al.* 1992, 1989).

As noted earlier, in the 1980s the suppliers of cocaine to US communities had more product than they could sell. The invention of crack cocaine helped them to market what otherwise was a very expensive product to a new group of consumers, poor urban drug users (Williams 1992). But unlike other drugs such as heroin that involved large capital investments to produce and transport the product to local retail markets, anyone with a small amount of powder cocaine could start their own neighborhood crack business. Consequently, the retail sale of crack in urban communities was run by large numbers of young "free-lance" dealers (Johnson *et al.* 1992). Operating independent of the social controls of either drug dealing hierarchies or the law, these young entrepreneurs routinely used violence to settle disputes with other dealers and customers over issues involving market share or product quality (Brownstein 1996). That is, there was violence related to crack cocaine and it was a product of disputes involving the system of crack trade and distribution, including disputes over sales territory, robberies of drug dealers and users, disputes over the quality of drugs being sold and purchased, disputes over drug paraphernalia, and so on (Goldstein *et al.* 1992, 1989; Riley 1997).

Naturally, the crack trade and the violence associated with it was not equally distributed across geographical or demographic boundaries and some people in some areas experienced the violence while others did not (Brownstein *et al.* 1992; Reinarman and Levine 1997; Reuter and Ebener 1992). But the fear spread across the city and across the country and criminal justice policymakers and law enforcement practitioners responded by getting tough. In terms of legislation, in 1986 the Narcotics Penalties and Enforcement Act was passed by Congress requiring that a *crack* dealer convicted of selling 5 grams of product receive the same sentence as a *powder* cocaine dealer convicted of selling 500 grams of what is essentially the same product. In terms of law enforcement, police departments followed a growing trend to shift from their traditional strategy of carefully building cases against middle and upper level drug dealers (Moore 1977) to a strategy that emphasized arresting large numbers of lower level dealers and users. For this new strategy they integrated the traditional methods of buy and bust, undercover surveillance, and stakeout operations (Chaiken 1988; Hayeslip 1989; Moore and Kleiman 1989; Sherman 1990) in a saturation model of policing that concentrated law enforcement resources and personnel over a period of time in an area of heavy drug trade to interdict the drug trafficking and disrupt the street sales in the area by arresting large numbers of drug dealers and users (Kleiman 1988; Zimmer 1987). Getting tough, unfortunately, had unintended consequences. Research that followed showed that it may have done more harm than good.

Saturation policing for street drug enforcement was on the rise when crack cocaine came to New York. Following the murder of a young police officer who was protecting a witness to a drug crime, in 1988 the New York City Police Department (NYPD) responded with its Tactical Narcotics Team (TNT) program. TNT was "[d]esigned to provide a short-term 'concentrated overlay' of street level drug enforcement in a narrowly defined target area [by supplementing] existing operations with intensive 'buy and bust' activity, focusing primarily on crack sales, but also addressing powdered cocaine and heroin trafficking" (Hillsman *et al.* 1989). An evaluation of TNT found no evidence of reduced criminal activity in areas targeted by the program, but did find that the people who participated in the crack markets in these areas "adapted to the intensive enforcement activity in a variety of ways" (Smith *et al.* 1992). In fact, the evaluators observed that dealers adapted by "moving selling locations indoors, shifting selling hours to times when it was believed that TNT might not be operating, by devising schemes to reduce hand-to-hand exchanges, by moving out of the selling location after a sale, by using 'observers' adept at spotting TNT vehicles, and by reducing the volume of outdoor sales for the duration of the intervention" (Smith *et al.*

1992: 141). So, for example, while doing little to reduce violent crime overall the get tough policy and saturation program did encourage the relocation of crack sales in time and space so that it became more difficult for law enforcement to observe and respond.

The TNT evaluation found that besides having limited potential to reduce crack-related crime and violence in an area, it might inadvertently have resulted in more rather than less violent crime. The evaluation found that many "curbside crack sellers who were arrested under the TNT program" were "quickly replaced by other user-dealers" (Smith et al. 1992: 141). Earlier research had shown that much of the violence related to crack was a product of disputes between crack dealers over territorial claims and that this market-related violence would decline once the legitimacy of such claims were recognized by local dealers (Goldstein et al. 1992). So by displacing dealers with recognized claims to specific territories, TNT disrupted the stability of the street trade and renewed the potentially violent competition over territorial rights (cf. Reuter 1991).

Other evaluations of saturation policing programs designed to address what was believed to be a crisis of crack cocaine similarly demonstrated that the program had limited ability to achieve its stated goal of controlling crack use and trade while having unintended consequences. For example, studies found that crime and violence in targeted areas was not being diminished but rather displaced, moving to neighboring areas until the intensive enforcement ended (Barnett 1988) and that while more arrests were being made, fewer prosecutions were successful (Bouza 1988). One study found that targeted raids by police of crack houses might have had a modest deterrent effect, but even that was likely to "decay" and "disappear" after being "mitigated by displacement" (Sherman et al. 1995: 776).

In Baltimore two astute observers of local street crack markets found that attempts to use street enforcement against local crack markets resulted in both displacement and increased violence (Simon and Burns 1997). In 1993 David Simon, formerly a crime reporter for the *Baltimore Sun* newspaper, and Edward Burns, formerly with the Baltimore Police Department, did the equivalent of an ethnographic study of the drug market in southwestern Baltimore and saw more cases of street violence after the police aggressively tried to move the market workers and operatives from their corners. Watching local police sweep the corners where the markets were located they observed:

> The crews migrate down the street and around the block ... The change in territory pushes competing products into proximity with each other, changing the distribution patterns. For years now, territory has been a dead concept in Baltimore's drug markets; anyone with a good product can set up shop, hire local fiends for touts, and share the same real estate as half a dozen other crews. But pressed by the police, the sprawl of the neighborhood drug bazaar is quickly compressed, so that more and more players—touts, slingers, stickup boys, burn artists—are hustling in a smaller space. There is a crossing of the corners' electrical currents: Dealers are more volatile than usual, the fiends, more desperate and nervous.
>
> *(Simon and Burns 1997: 217)*

They concluded that as a result of aggressive street enforcement against the crack dealers, "Violence picks up" (Simon and Burns 1997: 217).

Methamphetamine

Methamphetamine markets are not like crack markets. Crack cocaine is something users historically have purchased from strangers or casual acquaintances on street corners. Meth is something you buy from someone you know. Meth transactions are personal (Brownstein *et al.* 2012a). Late in the twentieth century in the US meth use was largely limited to states in the western part of the country and had consumers in rural as well as urban areas (National Institute of Justice 2003, 1999). At the time much of the production involved small local labs making meth for sale to people living nearby (Herz 2000; Hunt *et al.* 2005; Weisheit and White 2009). As meth began to spread and fear about related problems of health and safety increased, policymakers responded. And their response resulted in new ways of producing and distributing methamphetamine that made sure the demand was not unmet.

In the decades leading up to the twenty-first century methamphetamine was largely produced and distributed by local cooks who manufactured it in smaller quantities using precursor chemicals (e.g.

pseudoephedrine) readily available in the form of cold medicines and sold in local pharmacies and farming supply stores (National Drug Intelligence Center 2011, 2005). Around that time a number of studies of methamphetamine use and users were finding evidence of related public health and safety problems (CDC 2000; Hunt et al. 2005; Rodriquez et al. 2005; Sommers and Baskin 2004, 2006; Sommers et al. 2006; Weisheit and White 2009). Consequently the federal government policymakers were concerned (Office of National Drug Control Policy 2005) and the US Congress responded with passage of the Combat Methamphetamine Epidemic Act of 2005 (Title VII of the USA PATRIOT Improvement and Reauthorization Act of 2005, P.L. 109–77), with most states following with comparable legislation (McBride et al. 2011). The legislation was intended to regulate and control the sale of precursor chemicals needed to make meth in local labs including ephedrine, pseudoephedrine, and phenylpropanolamine to hinder the production of methamphetamine by the local cooks operating small production labs.

From 2007 to 2011 my colleagues and I conducted a national study of methamphetamine markets in America funded by the National Institute on Drug Abuse (R21DA024391). We conducted a mixed methods three-stage study including an exploratory screening survey of 1,367 police agencies across the country; open-ended, in-depth telephone interviews with 50 narcotics police in selected departments around the country; and visits to more than 28 cities and towns in five regions of the country (Southeast, Middle Atlantic, Midwest, Southwest, and Pacific Northwest). During our visits we observed and talked not only with local police but also with local and regional public health and safety officials, drug treatment and prevention workers, family service providers, meth users and dealers, and other people who know about meth markets in their community and region. Also, alone or with a guide we walked or drove through areas known to house meth users and dealers or to be a place where meth transactions occurred, and we attended community events where local citizens talked about personal and community issues and problems related to local meth use and markets. We also toured the US–Mexico border guided by a member of the US Border Patrol, following the fences and river and stopping at a border crossing.

A finding of our study of meth markets in America during the time after the passage of the legislation to combat meth was that there are different types and different mixes of types of markets in different locations, with some areas having no meth markets at all, though the markets are spreading (Brownstein et al. 2012b). Mainly, we found two types of markets. There were local mom-and-pop labs where a local cook uses what is sometimes a simple but always a dangerous technique to make enough meth to supply him- or herself and a few other people he or she knows with decent quality meth. The cook makes enough money to support his or her production and his or her livelihood. Then we found import markets with product mostly from Mexico arriving in the form of crystal meth to be sold through smaller scale local dealers selling to people they know, or to be warehoused for distribution throughout a region. We also found that areas with both mom-and-pop and import markets were more likely to report public health and safety problems than those with just one type of market (Taylor et al. 2011a, 2011b). Notably, we did not find much market-related violence in meth markets, though we did observe higher levels of violence and neglect in the families of people involved with methamphetamine users. But the main thing we learned is that in the US in the early twenty-first century, after the passage of federal and state legislation and policies to control and regulate methamphetamine use, the methamphetamine industry is thriving and perhaps stronger than it had been despite continuing public health and safety problems (Brownstein et al. 2012a, 2012b; Taylor et al. 2011a, 2011b). In fact, our findings demonstrate how now the methamphetamine industry in America is organized and operates, how it is linked to Mexican drug cartels, and how local retail meth markets are part of and integrally related to the national industry.

The passage of the Combat Methamphetamine Epidemic Act in 2005 inconvenienced the mom-and-pop labs that dominated the US meth market at the time making small amounts of meth for local users. But instead of closing down the industry it encouraged creative thinking and opened opportunities for entrepreneurial meth cooks and other illicit drug dealers to design and develop new ways to make and distribute meth. Studying this body of legislation and its impact, Duane McBride and his colleagues observed that states used a variety of approaches to reduce the availability of precursor drugs and while for the most part they initially reduced access to methamphetamine precursor drugs, in the longer term they did not all have the expected results (McBride et al.

2011). Our observations and interviews in communities across the country made it clear that while the legislation inconvenienced local meth labs in some places for some time, it also had the effect of motivating meth manufacturers and distributors to find new and innovative ways to bring their product to market. As one law enforcement officer we interviewed told us, "It's like playing checkers or chess. We make a move to counter, to investigate them, and they counter that move. And it's basically back and forth." So the methamphetamine industry in America grew and became more lucrative. In particular, there were two noteworthy responses to the attempts to regulate and control the industry with legislation and policy initiatives.

For local meth cooks, the problem was that they could no longer get the precursor chemicals they needed to manufacture meth. Before the legislation they could get the pseudoephedrine, for example, by purchasing large quantities of cold medicines that contained them from the shelves of any pharmacy. After the legislation the amount of cold medicine they could buy was limited, and worse still they had to identify themselves and leave a record of their purchase. So they invented what came to be known as "smurfing" (National Drug Intelligence Center 2009). Local meth cooks organized local users to go out and each purchase as much cold medicine as they could. Then they would get together with the cook and combine the limited supply of cold medicine available to each of them so the cook could prepare enough meth to meet their common need to get high. Today these gatherings operate much like the old mom-and-pop labs, with production and distribution centered on personal relationships, almost taking the form of a social club with family members, friends, or acquaintances from the surrounding community getting together at the home of their local neighborhood meth cook.

Related to the innovative use of smurfing to produce meth for local users is a technological development that simplified the process of making meth for local cooks and required less of the restricted ingredients. Local meth cooks developed a new technique that spread widely called one-pot or shake-and-bake (Washington University Law Review 2010). This technique is no less dangerous than the older methods of cooking meth and explosions still happen and toxic waste is still dumped. But the process is simpler and requires fewer resources. Shake-and-bake still requires pseudoephedrine, but not as much, and instead of anhydrous ammonia it uses ammonium nitrate from fertilizer or cold-pack compresses, which are not as hard to obtain (Blostein *et al.* 2009). Compared to the older anhydrous ammonia labs it makes less meth but requires less of easier to obtain precursor chemicals, it can more easily be made in a two-liter bottle (a large plastic soda pop bottle works well) almost anywhere (even a moving vehicle), and the production does not give off the easily identifiable odors emitted off by the older method. The cook can make enough meth to supply his regular customers in the two-liter soda bottle. He or she mixes the ingredients together combining them in the correct sequence in the two-liter bottle, shakes them, lets the gas out of the bottle being careful so that it does not explode, and serves the people sitting around waiting. Then everyone gets high. Anyone who wants to learn the details of this process can find recipes and instructions on the internet, including videos of people making meth using the shake-and-bake method. But as meth cooks told us, it can be dangerous so it helps to have a mentor who can teach you the proper way to make meth.

From interviews with police for our study of meth markets, we found that shake-and-bake presents them with problems that their traditional methamphetamine enforcement strategies cannot address and shortcomings in the policing tools previously available to them for investigating meth cases and enforcing laws against meth use and sales. For example, since shake-and-bake production does not give off the odor that came from production in the old mom-and-pop labs, it has become harder to find neighbors who recognize the odor and report it to the police. Since the production is mobile and can be done anywhere in a two-liter bottle, instead of seizures of lab equipment at a fixed and identifiable location now what police find are old toxic soda bottles lying on the side of the road. And just as the older labs sometimes exploded, the one-pot method also may result in an explosion.

On a larger scale and resulting in a more significant unintended negative consequence, following the 2005 Act and state legislation the illicit drug distributors working out of Mexico to bring heroin and cocaine into the US saw an opportunity to expand their product line to include methamphetamine (Beith 2010; Keefe 2012; Langton 2012). In many regions of the country these Mexican cartels came to dominate the local meth markets. In fact, most of the methamphetamine in the US today comes from so-called "super labs" primarily under the direction of Mexican drug cartels and organized to produce larger quantities of the product ("10 or more pounds of methamphetamine in a single production cycle") for wholesale distribution (National Drug Intelligence Center 2011: 23), though increasingly there is local smaller scale production in some areas of the country (National Drug Intelligence Center 2009). The super labs operated mostly but not exclusively by the Mexican cartels produce a higher quality crystal meth compared to the paste or powder produced by shake-and-bake. When they first arrived on the scene the Mexican importers experienced a problem reaching the local markets. Meth sales tend to be personal and they did not always have established personal relationships to work through. In places like the Pacific Northwest or Southwest where there are longstanding Mexican communities, the importers had a base through which to make the necessary contacts to open a local business. But in places like the Southeast and Middle Atlantic they did not. This problem was not insurmountable and in a short time a business solution was found. The local sales representatives sent to an area to establish a local retail business for the Mexican import organization would recruit local people with established ties to the local meth community to sell small quantities to local users on their behalf. In those parts of the country with established communities of Mexican people the local sellers might be Mexican. But in those places where local native white users might not be comfortable dealing with people they did not know who were recently arrived from Mexico, the importers would identify and set up a locally known and trusted native white user in a small retail business, sort of like a franchise, selling meth to other local native white users. With this business model the problem was solved.

Ill-informed policy and unintended consequences

The chemicals needed to make methamphetamine are found in everyday products, including things like cold medications and cleaning products. So it was not surprising in the early twenty-first century when methamphetamine use was considered a serious problem in the US that policy initiatives were introduced to limit access to those chemicals by controlling access to the household products in which they were found. What came as a bit of a surprise to those who viewed the problem in terms of control was that the policy had unintended consequences, some of which did more harm than good. The story about methamphetamine presented in this chapter took place in the US, but the problem of unintended consequences from unfounded meth policies is not limited to just that one nation.

When concerns about methamphetamine resulted in policies to control access to the chemicals needed to make meth, the impact of those policies did not end at US borders. Around that time the annual *World Drug Report* released by the United Nations concluded that as a result of the policy initiatives in North America to control access to precursor chemicals, production of methamphetamine shifted from the US to other parts of the world:

> The largest production areas for methamphetamine continue to be in South-East Asia, including Myanmar, China and the Philippines, and in North America. Traditionally, the majority of methamphetamine was produced in the USA, with the precursor chemicals smuggled into this country via Canada or Mexico. Improved controls in Canada and further tightening of controls in the USA has led to a decline in the number of clandestine laboratories operating within the United States and a shift of production across the border to Mexico. However, Mexico has now also improved its precursor control regime, prompting drug trafficking organizations to exploit other areas such as Central America and possibly Africa. In the Republic of South Africa, where methamphetamine is produced for the domestic market, both production and consumption have increased. The Oceania region, notably Australia and New Zealand, continue to be important producers and consumers of methamphetamine, but there are no indications that these drugs are exported.
>
> *(UNODC 2007: 123)*

In this way, the policy decisions and actions taken in one nation, the US, had unintended consequences for other nations.

But the US was not the only nation pursuing this drug policy before knowing what it might bring. Other nations and the international community similarly made meth policy on the basis of limited knowledge with comparable unintended consequences. In 2007 the United Nations Office on Drugs and Crime estimated that around the world there were between 15 and 16 million people using methamphetamine during the year (UNODC 2007: 17). This widespread use of methamphetamine was found despite earlier efforts by the United Nations to control access to chemicals needed to produce it. In 1988 in an Act passed at the United Nations Conference for the Adoption of a Convention Against Illicit Traffic in Narcotic Drugs and Psychotropic Substances, UN members agreed, "The Parties shall take the measures they deem appropriate to prevent diversion of substances in Table I [including pseudoephedrine] and Table II used for the purpose of illicit manufacture of narcotic drugs or psychotropic substances, and shall co-operate with one another to this end" (UN 1988: 12). Much of the resulting initiatives addressed the diversion of pseudoephedrine to keep it from people who would use it to make methamphetamine, at first on tighter restrictions on industrial producers and later more directly on consumer access through legitimate pharmaceutical products (McKetin 2007: 521). In an editorial in *Addiction*, Rebecca McKetin, who has conducted studies of methamphetamine markets in Australia (McKetin *et al.* 2005, 2006), concluded that while more research is still needed, "Successful precursor regulation may also have unintended consequences that need to be anticipated and managed. As regulation of precursor chemicals in wealthy destination markets become more stringent, responsibility for policing chemical diversion and synthetic drug manufacture and managing harms from synthetic drug use are likely to shift increasingly to developing countries—many of which have limited capacity to manage such problems" (McKetin 2007: 521).

It is bad enough when the unintended consequences of a policy result in a negative impact for the nation that established the policy, but even more troubling when resulting negative consequences take place in other nations. It is clear from the examples in this chapter that drugs have an international dimension and what one country does has consequences for other countries. Thus national solutions to domestic drug problems can be responsible for worsening drug-related problems or even creating new drug problems in other nations. This book began with a discussion of the problem of morphine, and showed how policies supported by ideological values and beliefs rather than knowledge derived from scientific analysis favored developed nations while creating problems for people, communities, businesses, and governments in developing nations. In this chapter, examples of cocaine and methamphetamine policies in developed nations, particularly the US but also others, similarly result in unintended and not necessarily desirable consequences in less developed or undeveloped nations.

When a nation experiences health and safety problems related to the use, misuse, or involvement of its people with drugs then it is certainly appropriate to respond with policies to address the problem. But the examples in this chapter show how the outcome of a policy can sometimes make things worse rather than better when the policy is not grounded in valid, reliable, and trustworthy evidence based on a comprehensive scientific analysis supported by sound theoretical principles. That is, for a policy to accomplish what it is intended to accomplish, it really is important to consider not only intended consequences but also unintended consequences.

6

FALSE ISSUES, DUBIOUS SOLUTIONS, AND THE NEED FOR PUBLIC DISCOURSE

Finding a definition of drugs is not as simple as it would seem. There are a number of federal agencies in the US that have some responsibility for drugs, so you might think they would define what they mean by "drugs." But a definition of drugs is not offered when the question is posed directly on their websites. Where the website offers the opportunity to search, enter the question: "What is a drug?" The Federal Drug Administration (FDA) site tells you that it uses investigations, compliance, enforcement, and criminal investigations in pursuit of its vision: "All food is safe; all medical products are safe and effective; and the public health is advanced and protected" (http://www.fda.gov/ICECI/Inspections/IOM/ucm124442.htm), so its website broadly defines drugs in terms of officially recognized "pharmacopoeia or formulary." The National Institute on Drug Abuse (NIDA) is a science agency that is organized to support research on drugs (http://www.drugabuse.gov/), so its website answers the question by directing you to read studies and reports on drugs of abuse. The Office of National Drug Control Policy (ONDCP) is a policy agency (http://www.whitehouse.gov/ondcp), so its website answers the question by suggesting you read policy reports and government documents on what the US government has been doing to fight and win the war on drugs. The Drug Enforcement Administration (DEA) is about enforcing drug laws (http://www.justice.gov/dea/), so its website suggests you read briefs, reports, and news accounts on actions taken against illicit drugs, drug use, and drug trafficking.

Perhaps it is not surprising then that a more useful way to find a precise and unambiguous definition of drugs is on the website of an organization intended to educate young people about the world around them and its people. For example, ask the question about the definition of drugs on the website of the Science Museum in London. In a few clicks you eventually find a page that specifically poses the question: "What is a drug?" The answer is: "A drug is any chemical you take that affects the way your body works." If that is not sufficient, another box on the page continues: "Alcohol, caffeine, aspirin and nicotine are all drugs. A drug must be able to pass from your body into your brain. Once inside your brain, drugs can change the messages your brain cells are sending to each other, and to the rest of your body. They do this by interfering with your brain's own chemical signals: neurotransmitters that transfer signals across synapses" (http://www.sciencemuseum.org.uk/WhoAmI/FindOutMore/Yourbrain/Howdodrugsaffectyourbrain/Whatisadrug.aspx). So the simple answer is that drugs are chemicals.

People use various chemical substances we commonly if too casually call drugs for lots of different reasons. Sometimes their use can be beneficial to the people using them and the people around them, and other times their use can be harmful. Lots of people just like using certain substances because the substance gives them pleasure or they believe the substance helps them relax or makes them feel more aware and appreciative of themselves and their surroundings (Huxley 1954; Marlatt 1996; O'Malley and Valverde 2004; Weil 1972). This could include a wide variety of substances from things like nicotine and caffeine to ecstasy and LSD. Some substances are popular sometimes among limited but nonetheless large segments of the population for recreational purposes, perhaps because they feel the substances enhance their social or intellectual skills or just help them to better enjoy their experiences with or even without other people around them (Brownstein *et al.* 2012a; Goode 2012; Ropero-Miller and Goldberger 1998). This could include substances like marijuana or alcohol but also methamphetamine or cocaine. And there are substances that people use for therapeutic purposes, to make them feel better or function better or just to get through a day of psychological or biological challenges to their comfort or well-being (Chou et al. 2009; Kalso and Vainio 1990; Mather 1995; Reisman 2011; WHO 2007). Substances used for this purpose could include those openly available in retail establishments, such as aspirin or naproxen; those legally produced by pharmaceutical companies and then distributed by prescription or recommendation through authorized medical providers, from diuretics to opiates and today even including marijuana in some places; and outlawed substances like heroin or cocaine, or legal substances distributed outside the law like oxycodone or dextroamphetamine.

So the chemical substances we call drugs can serve a social good and be good for people, and at the same time they can be a source of harm to users and the people around them, especially when they are used in inappropriate ways, in inharmonious settings or most notably when the substances by their properties in one way or another overpower the people using them. So having the substances we call drugs in our personal and social lives is not a simple matter. Unfortunately, given local beliefs and values and local politics and culture, contemporary drug policies around the world tend to trivialize and obfuscate the placement and role in our lives of this assortment of substances that sometimes can be good for us, sometimes bad for us, and sometimes both at the same time. When policymakers look at drugs simply as drugs and place them as a single category in a value-based and politicized context, they see and therefore address false issues and consequently design dubious solutions. Looking at the challenge of living with these substances from the perspective of the people for whom these substances pose a serious personal challenge, in particular addiction, Avram Goldstein wrote, "The misery suffered by addicts and their families is enormous. The costs to society—to all of us—are measured as loss of productivity, additional needs for medical care, dangers of drug-induced behaviors, destruction of family life, corruption of children, and burden on the criminal justice system. If we set aside political bombast, media sensationalism, and ill-informed calls for quick fixes, we can try—calmly and dispassionately—to examine what science can teach us about addictive drugs and addictive behavior. That requires a thorough analysis, drug by drug, of how each one acts and what harm each does to users and to society" (Goldstein 2001: 13). That is, to recognize the important issues and design appropriate solutions, even in perhaps the worst case we need to conduct thorough analyses of what is happening in terms of drug use and involvement and what consequences it is having on the people involved and the people around them, drug by drug and circumstance by circumstance.

Issues and solutions

The challenge for making drug policy is to understand how the various chemical substances we call drugs each and all relate to us psychologically and physiologically as individuals and socially and culturally as communities of people. We need to understand how they can contribute in positive ways to personal and social well-being and how they can be harmful to the health and safety of people and communities. Before we make decisions or take actions concerning how best to respond to what drugs do for us and to us, we need to better understand the consequences, intended and unintended, of those decisions and actions. Through our understanding we need to be able to explain what we are doing and why we are doing it. As discussed earlier, we build such explanations on what we know and then to fill the gaps in our knowledge we make assumptions about what we cannot know and speculate about what we have yet to learn with ideas drawn from ideology or theory or both.

For ideologues explanations are clouded by beliefs, opinions, attitudes, and values that support a particular favored position, so the collection and addition of new evidence is not necessarily of interest and sometimes even rejected. Even knowledge already supported by established evidence, particularly empirical evidence from scientific studies, may be ignored. Unsupportable assumptions may be taken as having equal value to scientific evidence. For social scientists and those interested in what can be learned through the scientific process of building new knowledge by testing ideas and accumulating evidence, assumptions that are made and the ways that gaps in knowledge are filled are dependent on the quality of available evidence and logic. Of course at its core theory is as dependent as ideology on assumptions, which cannot be proven or disproven by the techniques of scientific method. So the theory that is used as the basis for making the decisions and taking the actions that are the substance of policy, in this case drug policy, matters.

As discussed in earlier chapters, for contemporary drug policy there are policymakers who listen to ideologues making decisions and taking actions on the basis of their beliefs and values about people and society. They believe what they believe and value what they value, so no matter what evidence you present to them they are likely to stay the course. There are also policymakers who listen to social scientists and base their decisions and actions about drugs and drug policy on the basis of scientific evidence and the theory that supports them. They are more likely therefore to consider new evidence that enhances their explanation about the relationships between what we call drugs and the people who use them or are involved with them. The problem for contemporary drug policy is that even these policymakers who are receptive to new evidence and would be willing to consider new explanations have favored ideas from mainstream criminological theory.

Mainstream criminological theories, as discussed in earlier chapters, have tended to move drug policy in particular directions, notably favoring either repressive control and regulation programs and initiatives or compassionate but paternalistic harm-reduction programs and initiatives. Yet a drug problem remains in the sense that people and communities are still not getting the full benefit they could or should from the various substances we call drugs, and at the same time they are suffering the personal and social harms that the use and involvement with one or another of those substances can bring to them. It was also suggested in earlier chapters that critical criminological theories can move the discourse or debate on drug policy in new directions. This idea is not new and the direction was made clear almost two decades ago by Elliott Currie in his book on drugs and the problems of drugs particularly in the US when he wrote:

> There are two drug problems in America. One is the drug problem of the affluent. It is by no means insignificant, and it has caused more than its share of personal tragedies. But is a *manageable* [italics in the original] problem, and it has been steadily decreasing for several years, for reasons unrelated to the war on drugs. The other one is the drug problem of America's have-nots. That problem has grown malignantly in the face of the drug war – and it is much farther from solution than it was when the war began.
>
> *(Currie 1993: 3)*

Currie wrote those words around the time when crack cocaine was considered an epidemic in American cities and inner city communities faced with crack, heroin, PCP, and other drugs were declared to be in crisis. The hysteria over that crisis may since have passed, but the drug problem for poor people living in cities, and now also being recognized in rural areas, has not. Actually, neither has the problem for people who are not poor. We still need to figure out how to make what we call drugs contribute to the betterment of our lives while not making our lives worse. Critical criminological theories can be helpful in this regard by recognizing and bringing attention to the deeply rooted problems of society involving social distinctions such as race, class, and gender and by acknowledging the importance of social forces and arrangements of power, influence, and authority for decisions and actions that have an impact on particular people and particular communities in particular ways.

The need and opportunity for public discourse

In light of what we know, what we do not know, what we can theorize, and what we must assume about the substances we call drugs, it certainly can be argued that a comprehensive policy with a chance of being successful at addressing real problems while yielding benefits and not causing unnecessary harm would include both some elements of control or regulation and some elements of harm reduction. It is also reasonable to argue that the focus of the policy should be on maximizing the benefits and minimizing the harms of drug use and drug involvement, and not on the valuation of the worth of drugs, which are really only chemicals, or the people who use them or are involved with them. But to know what should be included in an overall policy that will have the greatest possible positive and least likely negative impact on people and society it is important first to know what the questions and the issues are and what kinds of solutions will likely lead to what kinds of consequences and outcomes. That is why an open and honest discourse and public debate is so important.

Policy-making is a complex process starting with discussion about whether or not there is a problem and what that problem is, setting an agenda to address the problem, formulating ideas, building support, implementing a strategy, and evaluating the results of implementation (Anderson 2011; Birkland 2011). Despite the fact that there is a record of some talk and writing about particular drug policies, notably legalization, or the overall impact of drug policy in general (e.g. Inciardi 1999; Trebach and Zeese 1990), to date the necessary discourse or debate on drug policy has yet to take place (cf. Drug Policy Alliance 2010; Gilmore 2012; Nadelmann 2004; Ryan 2012; Walker 2011). Advocates for different positions have made their voices heard. Advocates for particular policy directions have argued for policies in their favored direction. Ideologues have espoused positions favorable to their ideological bent. Social scientists have done research and provided theories and explanations building on research findings to support one policy direction or another. But advocates promote their favored positions to their constituents and followers. Ideologues do the same. Policymakers and politicians at all levels of government through the legislative process, public hearings, government reports, and the like talk mostly to each other and rarely listen to anyone else. Even when official public forums where the people making policy open their doors to the wider public are held, few people from the public get involved and come to listen and share ideas. Social scientists and theorists also have things to say, but they too talk to themselves, at their professional conferences and through their professional journals. So there are conversations taking place in public settings, but that is not necessarily the same thing as open and honest public discourse.

The news media could and should be a source of reaching the public with ideas and information about possible or pending policy decisions and actions, but they are less oriented to informing or engaging the public than they are to the business and politics of making a profit (Brownstein 1991a; Chancellor and Mears 1983; Curran et al. 2009; Gans 1979; Lee 1973). So newspapers, magazines, formal news websites, and the like would appear to have limited interest in serving this role. One interesting development involving news media in recent years is that with the advent of the internet, all news media to stay in business and reach any readers must have an online presence through a website. Anyone who reads a news article on a website has lots of opportunities to respond to the article through various cyber vehicles. Almost inevitably there are people who for no additional cost simply register with the website by providing real or false personal information so they can then submit a written comment in response to any article. This has serious potential to be a format for ongoing discourse or debate, but it is not yet set up for that purpose. If the news source really wanted to set up a serious discourse, they could do it, but the way in which it is set up leads to comments tending to come from anonymous people who are opinionated, angry, or otherwise moved to let people know what they think simply so they can see their words in print. There are examples of a few of these earlier in this book.

The opportunity for millions of people across the world to communicate quickly and directly as a result of the development and expansion of the internet does have promise. However, at the start of the twenty-first century we are still at the early stages of this form of human connection, and much of the way it is used has the feel of being experimental and even naïve. For example, through Facebook (http://www.facebook.com/) a person can reach out to "friends" and with a few keystrokes can share information (words, pictures, even video) and in a sense their feelings (i.e. "likes") with all and any of those friends. So a discussion could be generated among "friends," but only among friends and friends of friends. Through Twitter (https://twitter.com/) people can have "followers" rather than friends. Twitter calls itself an "information network" designed to provide "real-time information" connecting people with the latest news, opinions, and so on. Followers sign on to the accounts of the people they want to follow. This could be a source of ongoing sharing of information regarding the latest thinking on drug policy, but it would by design be one sided and in any case Twitter messages are limited to 140 characters. Another program called Reddit (http://www.reddit.com/) advertises itself as a vehicle through which people all over the world can share content and ideas and rate them as "good" or "junk." Anyone who registers can submit content and participants can form "communities" with a common interest in some area of content. So theoretically people interested in a serious discourse or debate over drug policy could start their own community. At this point this all is just a start. But these technologies are already showing promise in parts of the world where societies in turmoil are using them to help people communicate. As the social imagination of developers and users evolve over time the technology is there to host ongoing open discourse about serious topics, including drug policy.

At the start of the twenty-first century then we are living in a time when the possibility of a democratic open and just discourse on drug policy is possible, even at the international level. Combining the knowledge and experience of the ongoing scientific enterprise with the new technologies for communication could result in the kind of discourse or debate that needs to take place. Of course that would require that the people engaged in the exchange of ideas and words are willing to be open and honest, and that the vehicles for the exchange would have to be organized and operated to accept communications that allow participants to move beyond the constraints of the old cultural, social, and moral contexts that were supported by assumptions and ideologies grounded in a lack of knowledge and an inability of people to communicate.

Going forward

In writing about what were called drugs and the personal and social problems that were recognized as being associated with them at the end of the twentieth century, Currie argued that "it's past time we got on with the real job" (Currie 1993: 7). The purpose of his book is "to outline what it would take to launch a different kind of war, targeted at real enemies: the deeper roots of endemic drug abuse. That war will necessarily be a much tougher proposition than the quick-fix forays of the past twenty years, because it forces us to tackle deep-seated social and economic deficits we have let fester much too long" (Currie 1993: 7). That is, he was drawing our attention not only to the problems that were being related to what were called drugs but also to the impact of official drug policy, in particular the war on drugs, as it related differently to different people in different places in society. And he explained the need to devote our public resources and energy to defining and responding to these problems not by fighting symptoms but rather by understanding root causes. In that sense he was calling for a discourse on drug policy that would take its lead from critical criminological theory.

Around the time Currie's book was published, Ethan Nadelmann, who was widely recognized as a leading voice in the debate on legalization, acknowledged that it was time to shift attention to "create and advance a more informed and sophisticated public discourse about alternatives to drug prohibition—one that breaks free from the intellectual and moralistic confines of contemporary drug norms" (Nadelmann 1992: 85). So Currie was not alone. While Currie was calling for shifting the focus of our efforts to study and understand the drug problem, Nadelmann was calling for a shift specifically in the focus of public discourse on drug policy. Unfortunately, 20 years later neither the effort to study and understand drugs and related problems nor the effort to shift public discourse on drug policy has moved very far. Over the decades since that time in addition to the predictable government reports and proclamations there have been a number of books, articles, and reports written and published about drug policy. Some have been a bit more critical, but broadly the direction they set for research and the discourse on drugs continues to address drug policy primarily in terms of enforcement and interdiction (Falco 1996; Goode 2012; Kleiman *et al.* 2011; MacCoun and Reuter 1997) or harm reduction (Goldstein 2001; Goode 2012; Inciardi and Harrison 2000; Marlatt 1996; Nadelmann 2004; Riley and O'Hare 2000; Room and Reuter 2011). That is not to say that these writings individually do not introduce new ideas or that they favor the policies they write about, but rather that overall they do not shift the direction of the research or the discourse away from that set by mainstream theory focusing on narrow issues like legalization and harm reduction.

Over time across the world a number of politicians, researchers, and private citizens have been recognizing and speaking out on the failure of the war on drugs. Among numerous recent examples, on July 29, 2012 *The New York Times* reported in an article titled "South America Sees Drug Path to Legalization" that the president of Uruguay has called for a policy of regulated and controlled legal marijuana, and that in other South American nations similar policies are being considered (Cave 2012). Speaking at The Brookings Institution in Washington, DC on July 9, 2012, the Republican Governor of New Jersey, Chris Christie, said, "The war on drugs, while well-intentioned, has been a failure" (Becker 2012). In an editorial in the *South African Medical Journal* in February, 2011 the managing editor exclaimed, "The war on drugs has failed! Humans have always taken psychoactive substances and prohibition has never kept them from doing so" (Van Niekerk 2011: 80). In a forum article in an open source medical journal Canadian researchers wrote,

"Once widely supported, the 'war on drugs' has become increasingly controversial, as the political realization sinks in that it has wrought more harm than good" (Nickerson and Attaran 2012: 1). The Global Commission on Drug Policy is an association of organizations from around the world that are independently advocates for drug policy reform sharing the common goal of bringing "to the international level an informed, science-based discussion about humane and effective ways to reduce the harm caused by drugs to people and societies" (http://www.globalcommissionondrugs.org/what-we-do/). A recent report by the Commission opened, "The global war on drugs has failed, with devastating consequences for individuals and societies around the world. Fifty years after the initiation of the UN Single Convention on Narcotic Drugs, and 40 years after President Nixon launched the US government's war on drugs, fundamental reforms in national and global drug control policies are urgently needed" (Global Commission on Drug Policy 2011: 2).

It is not enough, however, to simply decry the failure of the war or to call for making policy changes. Given social and economic conditions and circumstances around the world today, if the goal is to make informed decisions based on science, now would be a good time for an open and honest discourse and debate about drug policy. But for it to truly help policymakers to move beyond the orthodox arguments for or against policy reform, the discourse would need to go beyond the predictable questions about things like legalization or harm reduction, or the difference between licit and illicit drugs. It would need first to more directly address root questions about knowledge, evidence, assumptions, and theory and explanation as they relate to how and why those various chemical substances we call drugs inevitably are part of our lives, for better and worse. Then it could address practical questions about how to respond, embracing the positive things that various chemical substances do for us and controlling or managing the negative things. It could then consider the consequences, intended and unintended, of particular responses to particular drugs and particular circumstances and to particular people. And perhaps most important it could consider what our responses accomplish for us in terms of public health and public safety, and what they say about us as people and as a society.

In the first chapter of this book reference was made to Cressey's prediction in the 1960s that criminology and criminologists in the US were poised to shift their attention to the study and understanding of the causal connections between criminal law, law enforcement, and violation (Cressey 1968), but instead given the dawning of the war on crime they became the "technical assistant(s) to politicians bent on repressing crime" (Cressey 1978: 173). Mainstream criminologists focused on the problem of crime rather than crime as a problem and seized the opportunity to pursue federal funding for research on what to do about crime (Cressey 1978: 171). An opportunity to use science to inform drug policy was lost. Reference was also earlier made to Currie's declaration in the early 1990s that we were at a point in history when given the contemporary status of the war on drugs it was time for social scientists to "question the root causes" of crime and drug abuse to better contribute to public policy (Currie 1993: 35). But the interests of mainstream criminologists interested in attacking the symptoms rather than addressing the causes of drug abuse prevailed (Currie 1993: 35). Again the search for root causes of drug abuse did not happen and again the opportunity for science to inform drug policy in a meaningful and productive way was lost. Now in the early twenty-first century once again we are at a point where policymakers and social scientists interested in making informed, realistic, productive, nonhazardous, just, and humane drug policy can shift their attention from a focus on the symptoms of drug use and drug involvement or how most efficiently to respond to observed or perceived negative consequences, to a focus on appreciating and understanding the intricacy of the place of the chemical substances we call drugs in our personal and social lives, the underlying reasons and root causes of how and why those various substances relate to our personal and social experience, and how they can sometimes be harmful and at other times beneficial to the people who use them and the people around them. The key will be to engage in an open and honest social discourse and public debate that would increase opportunities for new evidence to be found and evaluated, new ideas to be tested, and new policies to be tried and assessed.

REFERENCES

Akers, R.L. (2009) *Social Learning and Social Structure—A General Theory of Crime and Deviance*, New Brunswick, NJ: Transaction Publishers.
Akers, R.L. and Sellers, C.S. (2008) *Criminological Theories—Introduction, Evaluation, and Application* (5th edn), New York, NY: Oxford University Press.
Akers, R.L., Burgess, R.L. and Johnson, W.T. (1968) "Opiate use, addiction, and relapse," *Social Problems* 15: 459–69.
Alexander, B.K. (1990) *Peaceful Measures: Canada's Way Out of the War on Drugs*, Toronto: University of Toronto Press.
Anderson, J.E. (2011) *Public Policymaking* (7th edn), Boston, MA: Wadsworth.
Anderson, P. (1981) *High in America—The True Story Behind NORML and the Politics of Marijuana*, New York, NY: Viking Press.
Anderson, T. (2010) "The politics of pain," *British Medical Journal* 341: 328–30.
Anslinger, H.J. with Cooper, C.R. (1937) "Marijuana, assassin of youth," *The American Magazine* 124 (1), http://www.redhousebooks.com/galleries/assassin.htm (accessed May 26, 2012). Reprinted in Kaplan, J. (1971) *Marijuana—The New Prohibition*, New York, NY: Pocket Books.
Arrigo, B.A. and Bernard, T.J. (1997) "Postmodern criminology in relation to radical and conflict criminology," *Critical Criminology* 8: 39–60.
Aslan, R. (2008) "How opium can save Afghanistan," *The Daily Beast*, http://www.thedailybeast.com/articles/2008/12/19/how-opium-can-save-afghanistan.html (accessed April 5, 2012).
Attaran, A. and Boozary, A. (2011) "For peace and pain: the medical legitimization of Afghanistan's poppy crop," *Journal of Epidemiology and Community Health* 65: 396–98.
Austin, J. and McVey, D. (1989) "The 1989 NCCD prison population forecast: the impact of the war on drugs," *NCCD Focus*, Washington, DC: National Council on Crime and Delinquency.
Bakalar, J.B. and Grinspoon, L. (1984) *Drug Control in a Free Society*, Cambridge: Cambridge University Press.
Ball, J.C. and Ross, A. (1991) *The Effectiveness of Methadone Maintenance Treatment: Patients, Programs, Services, and Outcomes*, New York, NY: Springer-Verlag.

Barnett, A. (1988) "Drug crackdowns and crime rates: a comment on the Kleiman Report," in M.R. Chaiken (ed.), *Street-Level Drug Enforcement: Examining the Issues. Issues and Practices*, Washington, DC: US Department of Justice, pp. 35–42.

barr, s. (2011) "Needle-exchange programs face new federal funding ban," *Kaiser Health News*, http://www.kaiserhealthnews.org/stories/2011/december/21/needle-exchange-federal-funding.aspx (accessed July 2, 2012).

Baskin, D. and Sommers, I. (2006) "Methamphetamine use and violence," *Journal of Drug Issues* 36: 77–96.

Beccaria, C. (1963) *On Crimes and Punishment* (translated with an introduction by H. Paolucci), Indianapolis, IN: Bobbs-Merrill.

Becker, A. (2012) "Chris Christie calls war on drugs 'a failure'," *Huffington Post*, July 9, http://www.huffingtonpost.com/2012/07/09/chris-christie-drugs-war-on-drugs_n_1659687.html (accessed July 30, 2012).

Becker, H.S. (1963) *The Outsiders: Studies in the Sociology of Deviance*, New York, NY: Free Press.

Beith, M. (2010) *The Last Narco—Inside the Hunt for El Chapo, the World's Most Wanted Drug Lord*, New York, NY: Grove Press.

Bennett, T. (1988) "The British experience with heroin regulation," *Law and Contemporary Problems* 51: 299–314.

Berger, P.L. (1963) *Invitation to Sociology: A Humanistic Perspective*, Garden City, NY: Doubleday.

Berger, P.L. and Luckmann, T. (1966) *The Social Construction of Reality—A Treatise in the Sociology of Knowledge*, Garden City, NY: Doubleday & Company.

Bernard, T.J., Snipes, J.B. and Gerould, A.L. (2002) *Vold's Theoretical Criminology*, New York, NY: Oxford University Press.

Berridge, V. and Bourne, S. (2005) "Illicit drugs, infectious disease and public health: a historical perspective," *Canadian Journal of Infectious Diseases & Medical Microbiology* 16: 193–96.

Best, J. (1990) *Threatened Children—Rhetoric and Concern About Child Victims*, Chicago, IL: University of Chicago Press.

——(1989) *Images of Issues: Typifying Contemporary Social Problems*, New York, NY: Aldine de Gruyter.

Bewley-Taylor, D.R. (2003) "Challenging the UN drug conventions: problems and possibilities," *The International Journal of Drug Policy* 14: 171–79.

Biden, J.R., Jr (1990) *Fighting Drug Abuse: A National Strategy*, prepared by the Majority Staffs of The Senate Judiciary Committee and the International Narcotics Control Caucus, January.

Birkland, T.A. (2011) *An Introduction to the Policy Process—Theories, Concepts, and Models of Public Policy Making* (3rd edn), Armonk, NY: M.E. Sharpe.

Blostein, P.A., Plaisier, B.R., Maltz, S.B., Davidson, S.B., Wideman, E.W., Feucht, E.C. and VandenBerg, S.L. (2009) "Methamphetamine production is hazardous to your health," *The Journal of Trauma* 66: 1712–17.

Blumer, H. (1969) *Symbolic Interactionism—Perspective and Method*, Englewood Cliffs, NJ: Prentice-Hall.

Blumstein, A. and Beck, A.J. (1999) "Population growth in U.S. prisons, 1980–96," *Crime and Justice* 26: 17–61.

Bohm, R.M. and Vogel, B.L. (2011) *A Primer on Crime and Delinquency Theory*, Belmont, CA: Wadsworth.

Bourgois, P. (1995) *In Search of Respect—Selling Crack in El Barrio*, Cambridge: Cambridge University Press.

Bouza, A.V. (1988) "Evaluating street-level drug enforcement," in M.R. Chaiken (ed.), *Street-Level Drug Enforcement: Examining the Issues. Issues and Practices*, Washington, DC: US Department of Justice, pp. 43–48.

Brownstein, H.H. (2007) "How criminologists as social scientists can contribute to policy and practice," *Criminal Justice Policy Review* 18: 119–31.

——(2000) *The Social Reality of Violence and Violent Crime*, Boston, MA: Allyn & Bacon.

——(1998) "The drugs–violence connection: constructing policy from research findings," in E. Jensen and J. Gerber (eds), *The New War on Drugs: Its Construction and Impacts on Criminal Justice Policy in North America*, Cincinnati, OH: Anderson Publishing Company, pp. 59–69.

——(1996) *The Rise and Fall of a Violent Crime Wave—Crack Cocaine and the Social Construction of a Crime Problem*, Guilderland, NY: Harrow & Heston.

——(1992) "Making peace in the war on drugs," *Humanity and Society* 16: 217–35.

——(1991a) "The media and the construction of random drug violence," *Social Justice* 18: 85–103.

——(1991b) "Left realism and drug law enforcement," *The Critical Criminologist* 3: 1–2, 11–12.

——(1990) "Demilitarization of the war on drugs: toward an alternative drug strategy," in A.S. Trebach and K.B. Zeese (eds), *The Great Issues of Drug Policy*. Washington, DC: The Drug Policy Foundation, pp. 114–22.

Brownstein, H.H., Baxi, H.R.S., Goldstein, P.J. and Ryan, P.J. (1992) "The relationship of drugs, drug trafficking, and drug traffickers to homicide," *Journal of Crime and Justice* 15 (2): 25–44.

Brownstein, H.H., Mulcahy, T.M., Taylor, B.G., Fernandes-Huessy, J. and Hafford, C. (2012a) "Home cooking: marketing meth," *Contexts* 11: 30–35.

Brownstein, H.H., Mulcahy, T.M., Taylor, B.G., Fernandes-Huessy, J. and Woods, D. (2012b) "The organization and operation of illicit retail methamphetamine markets," *Criminal Justice Policy Review* 23: 67–89.

Butler, A. (2010) "Bad effects of drug abuse," August 3, http://www.livestrong.com/article/192397-bad-effects-of-drug-abuse/ (accessed July 4, 2012).

Cave, D. (2012) "South America sees drug path to legalization," *The New York Times*, July 29.

Centers for Disease Control and Prevention (CDC) (2010) "Syringe exchange programs—United States, 2008," *MMWR Morbidity and Mortality Weekly Report* 59: 1488–91.

——(2000) "Public health consequences among first responders to emergency events associated with illicit methamphetamine laboratories," *Weekly* 49: 1021–24.

Chafetz, J.S. (1978) *A Primer on the Construction and Testing of Theories of Sociology*, Itaska, IL: E.E. Peacock.

Chaiken, M.R. (1988) *Street-Level Drug Enforcement: Examining the Issues. Issues and Practices*, Washington, DC: US Department of Justice.

Chancellor, J. and Mears, W.R. (1983) *The News Business*, New York, NY: Harper and Row.

Chaplin, R., Flatley, J. and Smith, K. (2011) *Crime in England and Wales 2010/11—Findings from the British Crime Survey and Police Recorded Crime* (2nd edn), Home Office Statistical Bulletin, London: Home Office Statistics.

Chou, R., Ballantyne, J.C., Fanciullo, G.J., Fine, P.G. and Miaskowski, C. (2009) "Research gaps on use of opioids for chronic noncancer pain: findings from a review of the evidence for an American Pain Society and American Academy of Pain Medicine Clinical Practice Guideline," *The Journal of Pain* 10: 147–59.

Chouvy, P-A. (2008) "Licensing Afghanistan's opium: solution or fallacy?," *Caucasian Review of International Affairs* 2: 1–6.

Christie, N. (1981) *The Limits of Pain*, Irvington-on-Hudson, NY: Columbia University Press.

Chu, L.F., Clark, D.J. and Angst, M.S. (2006) "Opioid tolerance and hyperalgesia in chronic pain patients after one month of oral morphine therapy: a preliminary prospective study," *The Journal of Pain* 7: 43–48.

Cloward, R. and Ohlin, L. (1960) *Delinquency and Opportunity*, Glencoe, IL: Free Press.

Cohen, A.K. (1955) *Delinquent Boys*, Glencoe, IL: Free Press.

Cohen, P. (1996) "The case of two Dutch drug policy commissions—an exercise in harm reduction 1968–76," paper presented at the 5th Annual International Conference on the Reduction of Drug related Harm, March 7–11, 1994, Toronto: Addiction Research Foundation. Revised in 1996, http://dare.uva.nl/document/12561 (accessed May 28, 2012).

Cooley, C.H. (1922) *Human Nature and Social Order*, New York, NY: Charles Scribner's Sons.

Cornish, D.B. and Clarke, R.V. (1986) *The Reasoning Criminal: Rational Choice Perspectives on Offending*, New York, NY: Springer.

Cressey, D.R. (1978) "Criminological theory, social science, and the repression of crime," *Criminology* 16: 171–91.

——(1968) "Negotiated justice," *Criminologica* 5: 5–16.

Curran, D.J. and Renzetti, C.M. (2001) *Theories of Crime*, Boston, MA: Allyn & Bacon.

Curran, J., Iyengar, S., Brink Lund, A. and Salovaara-Moring, I. (2009) "Media system, public knowledge and democracy—a comparative study," *European Journal of Communication* 24: 5–26.

Currie, E. (1993) *Reckoning—Drugs, the Cities, and the American Future*, New York, NY: Hill and Wang.

Curtis, L.A. (1989) *The National Drug Control Strategy and Inner City Policy*, Testimony Before the Select Committee on Narcotics Abuse and Control,

United States House of Representatives, November 15, 1989. Washington, DC: Milton Eisenhower Foundation.

DeKeseredy, W.S. (2011) *Contemporary Critical Criminology*, London and New York, NY: Routledge.

——(2003) "Left realism on inner-city violence," in M.D. Schwartz and S.E. Hatty (eds), *Controversies in Critical Criminology*, Cincinnati, OH: Anderson Publishing, pp. 29–42.

DeKeseredy, W.S. and Dragiweicz, M. (2012) *Routledge Handbook of Critical Criminology*, London and New York, NY: Routledge.

Denno, D.W. (1988) "Human biology and criminal responsibility: free will or free ride?," *University of Pennsylvania Law Review* 137: 615–71.

Denzau, A.T. and Munger, M.C. (1986) "Legislators and interest groups: how unorganized interests get represented," *American Political Science Review* 80: 89–103.

Des Jarlais, D.C. (2000) "Research, politics, and needle exchange," *American Journal of Public Health* 90: 1392–94.

——(1996) "Editorial: harm reduction—a framework for incorporating science into drug policy," *American Journal of Public Health* 85: 10–12.

Dobkin, C. and Nicosia, N. (2009) "The war on drugs: methamphetamine, public health, and crime," *American Economic Review* 99: 324–49.

Drug Policy Alliance (2010) *Making Your Voice Heard—2010 Annual Report*, New York, NY: Drug Policy Alliance.

DuPont, R.L. and Voth, E.A. (1995) "Drug legalization, harm reduction, and drug policy," *Annual Internal Medicine* 123: 461–65.

Durkheim, E. (1933) *The Division of Labor in Society* (translated by G. Simpson), New York, NY: Free Press.

Duster, T. (1970) *The Legislation of Morality—Law, Drugs, and Moral Judgment*, New York, NY: Free Press.

Einstadter, W.J. and Henry, S. (2006) *Criminological Theory: An Analysis of its Underlying Assumptions*, Lanham, MD: Rowman & Littlefield.

Erickson, P.G. and Hathaway, A.D. (2010) "Normalization and harm reduction: research avenues and policy agendas," *International Journal of Drug Policy* 21: 137–39.

Falco, M. (1996) "U.S. drug policy: addicted to failure," *Foreign Policy* 102: 120–33.

Federal Bureau of Investigation (FBI) (2011) *Crime in the United States 2010*, Washington, DC: US Department of Justice, http://www.fbi.gov/about-us/cjis/ucr/crime-in-the-u.s/2010/crime-in-the-u.s.-2010 (accessed July 9, 2012).

Ferrell, J. (2003) "Cultural criminology," in M.D. Schwartz and S.E. Hatty (eds), *Controversies in Critical Criminology*, Cincinnati, OH: Anderson Publishing, pp. 71–84.

Ferrell, J. and Sanders, C.R. (1995) *Cultural Criminology*, Boston, MA: Northeastern University Press.

Fishbein, D.H. (1990) "Biological perspectives in criminology," *Criminology* 28: 27–72.

Fuhrman, E.R. (1989) "Reflexivity and Alvin Gouldner: the coming crisis in 1990," *The American Sociologist* 20: 357–61.
Gans, H.J. (1979) *Deciding What's News—A Study of CBS Evening News, NBC Nightly News, Newsweek, and Time*, New York, NY: Pantheon.
Gauchat, G. (2012) "Politicization of science in the public sphere: a study of public trust in the United States, 1974 to 2010," *American Sociological Review* 77: 167–87.
General Accounting Office (1993) *Needle Exchange—Research Suggests Promise as an AIDS Prevention Strategy*, Washington, DC: Report to the Chairman, Select Committee on Narcotics Abuse and Control, House of Representatives.
Gibbs, J.P. (1987) "The state of criminological theory," *Criminology* 25: 821–40.
Gilmore, I.T. (2012) "Drug policy debate is needed," *British Medical Journal* 344: e2381.
Global Commission on Drug Policy (2011) *Report of the Global Commission on Drug Policy*, http://www.globalcommissionondrugs.org/Report (accessed July 30, 2012).
Goldstein, A. (2001) *Addiction: From Biology to Drug Policy* (2nd edn), New York, NY: Oxford University Press.
Goldstein, P.J., Brownstein, H.H., Ryan, P.J. and Bellucci, P.A. (1989) "Crack and homicide in New York City, 1988: a conceptually-based event analysis," *Contemporary Drug Problems* 16: 651–87.
Goldstein, P.J., Brownstein, H.H. and Ryan, P.J. (1992) "Drug-related homicide in New York: 1984 and 1988," *Crime and Delinquency* 38: 459–76.
Goode, E. (2012) *Drugs in American Society*, Boston, MA: McGraw Hill.
Gottfredson, M. and Hirschi, T. (1990) *A General Theory of Crime*, Palo Alto, CA: Stanford University Press.
Gouldner, A.W. (1970) *The Coming Crisis of Western Sociology*, New York, NY: Basic Books.
Hamilton, M.B. (1987) "The elements of the concept of ideology," *Political Studies* 35: 18–38.
Hantman, J.A. (1995) "Research on needle exchange: redefining the agenda," *Bulletin of the New York Academy of Medicine* Winter: 397–412.
Hayeslip, D.W. (1989) "Local-level drug enforcement: new strategies," in *NIJ Reports. Research in Action*, March/April, Washington, DC: National Institute of Justice, pp. 2–7.
Herz, D. (2000) *Drugs in the Heartland: Methamphetamine in Rural Nebraska. Research in Brief*, Washington, DC: National Institute of Justice.
Hillsman, S.T., Sadd, S., Sullivan, M.L. and Sviridoff, M. (1989) *The Community Effects of Street Level Narcotics Enforcement: A Study of the New York City Police Department's Tactical Narcotic Teams*, New York, NY: Vera Institute.
Hirschi, T. (1969) *Causes of Delinquency*, Berkeley, CA: University of California Press.
Humphrey, E.S. (1991) *Drug Offenders Committed to State Prison*, Albany, NY: New York State Department of Correctional Services.

Hunt, D.E., Kuck, S. and Truitt, L. (2005) *Methamphetamine Use: Lessons Learned*, report submitted to the National Institute of Justice, Cambridge, MA: Abt Associates.

Hurley, S.F., Jolley, D.J. and Kaldor, J.M. (1997) "Effectiveness of needle-exchange programmes for prevention of HIV infection," *The Lancet* 349: 1797–800.

Husch, J.A. (1992) "Culture and US drug policy: toward a new conceptual framework," *Daedalus* 121: 293–304.

Huxley, A. (1954) *Doors of Perception*, New York, NY: Harper and Row.

Inciardi, J.A. (2007) *War on Drugs IV: The Continuing Saga of the Mysteries and Miseries of Intoxication, Addiction, Crime and Public Policy* (4th edn), Boston, MA: Allyn & Bacon.

——(ed.) (1999) *The Drug Legalization Debate* (2nd edn), Thousand Oaks, CA: Sage Publications.

Inciardi, J.A. and Harrison, L.D. (eds) (2000) *Harm Reduction—National and International Perspectives*, Thousand Oaks, CA: Sage.

Inciardi, J.A., Lockwood, D. and Pottieger, A.E. (1993) *Women and Crack Cocaine*, New York, NY: MacMillan.

International Narcotics Control Board (INCB) (2003) *Report of the International Narcotics Control Board for 2003*, Vienna: United Nations.

Ismaili, K. (2006) "Contextualizing the criminal justice policy-making process," *Criminal Justice Policy Review* 17: 255–69.

Jacoby, J.E. (2004) *Classics of Criminology*, Prospect Heights, IL: Waveland Press.

Johnson, B.D., Hamid, A. and Sanabria, H. (1992) "Emerging models of crack distribution," in T. Mieczkowski (ed.), *Drugs, Crime, and Social Policy: Research, Issues, and Concerns*, Boston, MA: Allyn & Bacon, pp. 56–78.

Joint Committee on New York Drug Law Evaluation (1977) *The Nation's Toughest Drug Law: Evaluating the New York Experience. Final Report*, New York, NY: The Association of the Bar of the City of New York, Drug Abuse Council, Inc.

Joseph, H., Stancliff, S. and Langrod, J. (2000) "Methadone maintenance treatment (MMT): a review of historical and clinical issues," *The Mount Sinai Journal of Medicine* 67: 347–64.

Kaiser, J. (2003) "NIH roiled by inquiries over grants hit list," *Science* 302: 758.

Kalso, E. and Vainio, A. (1990) "Morphine and oxycodone hydrochloride in the management of cancer pain," *Clin Pharmacol Ther* 47: 639–46.

Kaplan, J. (1971) *Marijuana—The New Prohibition*, New York, NY: Pocket Books.

Keefe, P.R. (2012) "Cocaine incorporated," *New York Times Magazine*, June 15: 36–43, 62–63.

Kestin, I. (1993) "Morphine," *Pharmacology* 3: Article 6, http://www.nda.ox.ac.uk/wfsa/html/u03/u03_016.htm (accessed April 18, 2012).

Kleiman, M.A.R. (1992) *Against Excess—Drug Policy for Results*, New York, NY: Basic Books.

——(1988) "Crackdowns—the effects of intensive enforcement on retail heroin dealing," in M.R. Chaiken (ed.), *Street-Level Drug Enforcement:*

References

Examining the Issues. Issues and Practices, Washington, DC: US Department of Justice, pp. 3–34.

Kleiman, M.A.R., Caulkins, J.P. and Hawken, A. (2011) *Drugs and Drug Policy: What Everyone Needs to Know*, New York, NY: Oxford University Press.

Koob, G.F. and Volkow, N.D. (2010) "Neurocircuitry of addiction," *Neuropsychopharmacology Reviews* 35: 217–38.

Kuhn, T.S. (1977) "Objectivity, value judgment, and theory choice," in T.S. Kuhn (ed.), *The Essential Tension: Selected Studies in the Scientific Tradition*, Chicago, IL: University of Chicago Press.

Langton, J. (2012) *Gangland—The Rise of the Mexican Drug Cartels from El Paso to Vancouver*, Mississauga, Ontario: Wiley & Sons Canada.

Lee, A.M. (1973) *The Daily Newspaper in America—The Evolution of a Social Instrument*, New York, NY: Octagon Books.

Leiss, W. (1975) "Ideology and science," *Social Studies of Science* 5: 193–201.

Lemert, E.M. (1967) *Human Deviance, Social Problems, and Social Control*, Englewood Cliffs, NJ: Prentice Hall.

Leshner, A.I. (2003) "Editorial: don't let ideology trump science," *Science* 302: 1479.

Lilly, J.R., Cullen, F.T. and Ball, R.A. (2011) *Criminological Theory* (5th edn), Thousand Oaks, CA: Sage.

Lindesmith, A.R. (1973) "Narcotic lobby and the drug problem," *Valparaiso University Law Review* 8: 591–614.

——(1957) "The British system of narcotics control," *Law and Contemporary Problems* 22: 138–54.

——(1938) "A sociological theory of drug addiction," *American Journal of Sociology* 43: 593–613.

Literary Digest (1929) "Government farms for drug addicts," *The Literary Digest* 103: 28, http://www.unz.org/Pub/LiteraryDigest-1929nov02–00028 (accessed May 28, 2012).

Lombroso-Ferrero, G. and Savitz, L. (1972) *Criminal Man, According To The Classification Of Cesare Lombroso* (original by G. Lombroso-Ferrerro, 1911, Publication No. 134, Introduction by L. Savitz), Montclair, NJ: Patterson Smith.

Lurie, P., Reingold, A.L., Bowser, B., Chen, D., Foley, J., Guydish, J., Kahn, J.G., Lane, S. and Sorensen, J. (1993) *Public Health Impact of Needle Exchange Programs in the United States and Abroad: Summary, Conclusions, and Recommendations*, NCJ 165664, Atlanta, GA: Centers for Disease Control and Prevention.

Lynch, M. (2012) "Theorizing the role of the 'war on drugs' in US punishment," *Theoretical Criminology* 16: 175–99.

McBride, D.C., Terry-McElrath, Y.M., Chriqui, J.F., O'Connor, J.C., VanderWaal, C.J. and Mattson, K.L. (2011) "State methamphetamine precursor policies and changes in small toxic lab methamphetamine," *Journal of Drug Issues* Fall: 253–82.

MacCoun, R. and Reuter, P. (1997) "Interpreting Dutch cannabis policy: reasoning by analogy in the legalization debate," *Science* 278: 47–52.

McKetin, R. (2007) "Methamphetamine precursor regulation: are we controlling or diverting the drug problem?," *Addiction* 103: 521–23.

McKetin, R., McLaren, J. and Kelly, E. (2005) *The Sydney Methamphetamine Market: Patterns of Supply, Use, Personal Harms and Social Consequences*, Monograph Series No. 13, National Drug Law Enforcement Research Fund, Sydney: National Alcohol and Drug Research Centre.

McKetin, R., McLaren, J., Riddell, S. and Robins, L. (2006) "The relationship between methamphetamine use and violent behavior," *Crime and Justice Bulletin*. Sydney: NSW Bureau of Crime Statistics and Research.

MacLean, B.D. (1993) "Left realism, local crime surveys and policing of racial minorities," *Crime, Law and Social Change* 19: 51–86.

McPhee, S.J., Papadakis, M. and Rabow, M.W. (2012) *Current Medical Diagnosis and Treatment* (51st edn), New York, NY: McGraw Hill.

McWilliams, J.C. (1990) *The Protectors: Harry J. Anslinger and the Federal Bureau of Narcotics*, Newark, DE: University of Delaware.

Maestro, M. (1973) *Cesare Beccaria and the Origins of Penal Reform*, Philadelphia, PA: Temple University Press.

Malinowska-Sempruch, K. (2012) "Sensible drug policies: will evidence finally overtake prejudice?," *Huffington Post*, Politics, United Kingdom, July 12, http://www.huffingtonpost.co.uk/kasia-malinowskasempruch/sensible-drug-policies-wi_b_1688560.html?view=screen (accessed July 21, 2012).

Marlatt, G.A. (1996) "Harm reduction: come as you are," *Addictive Behaviors* 21: 779–88.

Mather, L.E. (1995) "1994 John J. Bonica Lecture: the clinical effects of morphine pharmacology," *Regional Anesthesia* 20: 263–82.

Matthews, R. (1987) "Taking realist criminology seriously," *Contemporary Crises* 11: 371–401.

Mead, G.H. (1934) *Mind, Self, and Society*, Chicago, IL: University of Chicago Press.

Meisler, S. (1996) "The first drug czar," *The Drug Policy Letter* 29: 13–17. (Originally published in *The Nation* February 20, 1962.)

Merton, R.K. (1938) "Social structure and anomie," *American Sociological Review* 3: 672–82.

Michalowski, R.J. (1990) "Crime and justice in socialist Cuba: what can left realism learn?," paper presented at the Conference on Realist Criminology, May 24–25, Vancouver, British Columbia.

Miller, G. and Holstein, J.A. (1993) "Constructing social problems: context and legacy," in G. Miller and J.A. Holstein (eds), *Constructionist Controversies—Issues in Social Problems Theory*, New York, NY: Aldine de Gruyter, pp. 3–18.

Moore, M.H. (1977) *Buy and Bust—The Effective Regulation of an Illicit Heroin Market*, Lexington, MA: Lexington Books.

Moore, M.H. and Kleiman, M.A.R. (1989) "The police and drugs," *Perspectives on Policing*, September, Washington, DC: National Institute of Justice.

Moss, A.R. (2000) "Epidemiology and the politics of needle exchange," *American Journal of Public Health* 90: 1385–87.

Musto, D. (1999) *The American Disease* (3rd edn), New York, NY: Oxford University Press.

——(1991) "Opium, cocaine, and marijuana in American history," *Scientific American* 265: 40–47.

Nadelmann, E.A. (2007) "Drugs," *Foreign Policy* 162: 24–26, 28, 30.

——(2004) "Criminologists and punitive drug prohibition: to serve or challenge?" *Criminology and Public Policy* 3: 441–50.

——(1992) "Thinking seriously about alternatives to drug prohibition," *Daedalus* 121: 85–132.

——(1989) "Drug prohibition in the United States: costs, consequences, and alternatives," *Science* 245: 939–94.

National Drug Intelligence Center (2011) *National Drug Threat Assessment 2010*, No. 2011-Q0317–001, Washington, DC: US Department of Justice.

——(2009) *Pseudoephedrine smurfing fuels surge in large-scale methamphetamine production in California*, Situation Report, Product No. 2009-S0787–007, Washington, DC: US Department of Justice.

——(2005) *Methamphetamine Drug Threat Assessment*, No. 2005-Q0317–009, Washington, DC: US Department of Justice.

National Institute of Justice (2003) *2000 Arrestee Drug Abuse Monitoring: Annual Report*, NCJ 193013, Washington, DC: US Department of Justice.

——(1999) *Meth Matters: Report on Methamphetamine Users in Five Western Cities*, NCJ 176331, Washington, DC: US Department of Justice.

Newcomb, M.D. (1992) "Substance abuse and control in the United States: ethical and legal issues," *Social Science & Medicine* 35: 471–79.

Newcombe, R. (1992) "The reduction of drug related harm: a conceptual framework for theory, practice and research," in P.A. O'Hare, R. Newcombe, A. Matthews, E.C. Buning and E. Drucker (eds), *The Reduction of Drug Related Harm*, London: Routledge, pp. 1–14.

Nickerson, J.W. and Attaran, A. (2012) "The inadequate treatment of pain: collateral damage from the war on drugs," *PLoS Medicine* 9(1): e1001153, doi:10.1371/journal.pmed.1001153 (accessed July 30, 2012).

Office of the Attorney General (1989) *Drug Trafficking—A Report to the President of the United States*, Washington, DC: US Department of Justice.

Office of Justice Research and Performance (2010a) *New York State Felony Drug Arrest, Indictment and Commitment Trends, 1973–2008*, Albany, NY: Division of Criminal Justice Services.

——(2010b) *Preliminary Impact of 2009 Drug Law Reform, October 2009–September 2010*, Albany, NY: Division of Criminal Justice Services.

Office of National Drug Control Policy (ONDCP) (2012a) *National Drug Control Strategy*, Washington, DC: The White House.

——(2012b) *FY 2013 Budget and Performance Summary—Companion to the National Drug Control Strategy*, Washington, DC: The White House.

——(2011) *ADAM II—2010 Annual Report, Arrestee Drug Abuse Monitoring Program II*, Washington, DC: The White House.

——(2005) *National Drug Control Strategy*, Washington, DC: The White House.

——(1990) *National Drug Control Strategy*, Washington, DC: The White House.

——(1989) *National Drug Control Strategy*, Washington, DC: The White House.
O'Malley, P. and Valverde, M. (2004) "Pleasure, freedom and drugs: the uses of 'pleasure' in liberal governance of drug use and alcohol consumption," *Sociology* 38: 25–42.
Pepinsky, H.E. (1991) *The Geometry of Violence and Democracy*, Bloomington, IN: Indiana University Press.
——(1987) "Information sharing as a human right," *Humanity and Society* 11: 189–211.
——(1986) "This can't be peace: a pessimist looks at punishment," in G. Newman (ed.), *Punishment and Privilege*, New York, NY: Harrow and Heston, pp. 119–30.
Pepinsky, H.E. and Jesilow, P. (1984) *Myths That Cause Crime*, Cabin John, MD: Seven Locks Press.
Pepinsky, H.E. and Quinney, R. (1991) *Criminology as Peacemaking*, Bloomington, IN: Indiana University Press.
Pergolizzi, J., Boger, R.H., Budd, K., Dahan, A., Erdine, S., Hans, G., Kress, H.-G., Langford, R., Likar, R., Raffa, R.B. and Sacerdote, P. (2008) "Opioids and the management of chronic severe pain in the elderly: consensus statement of an international expert panel with focus on the six clinically most often used World Health Organization step III opioids (Buprenorphine, Fentanyl, Hydromorphone, Methadone, Morphine, Oxycodone)," *Pain Practice* 8: 287–313.
Pizzo, P.A. and Clark, N.M. (2012) "Alleviating suffering 101—pain relief in the United States," *New England Journal of Medicine* 366: 197–99.
Popper, K.R. (1959) *The Logic of Scientific Discovery*, New York, NY: Routledge.
Provine, D.M. (2011) "Race and inequality in the war on drugs," *Annual Review of Law and Social Science* 7: 41–60.
Quinney, R. (1970) *The Social Reality of Crime*, Boston, MA: Little Brown.
Reckless, W. (1961) "A new theory of delinquency and crime," *Federal Probation* 25: 42–46.
Reinarman, C. and Levine, H.G. (1997) "Crack in context—America's latest demon drug," in C. Reinarman and H.G. Levine (eds), *Crack in America—Demon Drugs and Social Justice*, Berkeley, CA: University of California Press, pp. 1–17.
——(1990) "A peace movement has emerged against the war on drugs," *ASA Footnotes* February: 3, 9.
Reisman, S.E. (2011) "New lead for pain treatment," *Nature* 471: 458–59.
Reiss, A.J. (1951) "Delinquency as the failure of personal and social controls," *American Sociological Review* 16: 196–207.
Reuter, P.H. (1992) "Hawks ascendant: the punitive trend of American drug policy," *Daedalus* 121: 15–52.
——(1991) "On the consequences of toughness," *A RAND Note*, N-3447-DPRC: 138–64.
Reuter, P.H. and Ebener, P.A. (1992) *Cocaine: The First Decade*, RAND Drug Policy Research Center Issue Paper, April, Santa Monica, CA: The RAND Drug Policy Research Center.

Reuter, P.H. and Stevens, A. (2007) *An Analysis of UK Drug Policy—A Monograph Prepared for the UK Drug Policy Commission*, London: UK Drug Policy Commission.

Riley, D. and O'Hare, P. (2000) "Harm reduction: history, definition, and practice," in J.A. Inciardi and L.D. Harrison (eds), *Harm Reduction—National and International Perspectives*, Thousand Oaks, CA: Sage, pp. 1–26.

Riley, D., Sawka, E., Conley, P., Hewitt, D., Mitic, W., Poulin, C., Room, R., Single, E. and Topp, J. (1999) "Harm reduction: concepts and practice. A policy discussion paper," *Substance Use and Misuse* 34: 9–24.

Riley, J.K. (1997) *Crack, Powder Cocaine, and Heroin: Drug Purchase and Use Patterns in Six U.S. Cities*, Washington, DC: National Institute of Justice.

Rodriquez, N., Katz, C., Webb, V.J. and Schaefer, D.R. (2005) "Examining the impact of individual, community, and market factors on methamphetamine use: a tale of two cities," *Journal of Drug Issues* Fall: 665–93.

Room, R. and Reuter, P. (2011) "How well do international drug conventions protect public health?," *The Lancet* 279: 84–91.

Ropero-Miller, J.D. and Goldberger, B.A. (1998) "Recreational drugs: current trends in the 90s," *Clinics in Laboratory Medicine* 18: 727–46.

Ross, E.A. (1901) *Social Control: A Survey of the Foundations of Order*, New York, NY: Macmillan.

Ross, R.A. and Cohen, M. (1988) *New York State: Trends in Felony Drug Offense Processing 1983–1987*, Albany, NY: New York State Division of Criminal Justice Services.

Rubin, B.R. (2000) "The political economy of war and peace in Afghanistan," *World Development* 28: 1789–803.

Ryan, J. (2012) "We need to have a more productive debate on drug laws," *Canberra Times*, June 29, http://www.canberratimes.com.au/opinion/we-need-to-have-a-more-productive-debate-on-drug-laws-20120628-2155y.html (accessed July 26, 2012).

Schneider, A. and Ingram, H. (1990) "Behavioral assumptions of policy tools," *The Journal of Politics* 52: 510–29.

Schutz, A. (1962) *Collected Papers I. The Problem of Social Reality* (edited with an Introduction by W. Natanson), The Hague: Martinus Nijhoff.

Schwartz, M.D. (1989) "The undercutting edge of criminology," *The Critical Criminologist* 1: 1–2, 5.

Schwartz, M.D. and Hatty, S.E. (2003) *Controversies in Critical Criminology*, Cincinnati, OH: Anderson.

Shaw, C. and McKay, H.D. (1942) *Juvenile Delinquency and Urban Areas*, Chicago, IL: University of Chicago Press.

Sherman, L.W. (1990) "Police crackdowns," *NIJ Reports. Research in Action*, Washington, DC: National Institute of Justice.

Sherman, L.W., Rogan, D.P., Edwards, T., Whipple, R., Shreve, D., Witcher, D., Trimble, W., Velke, R., Blumberg, M., Beatty, A. and Brideforth, C. A. (1995) "Deterrent effects of police raids on crack houses: a randomized, controlled experiment," *Justice Quarterly* 12: 755–81.

Simon, D. and Burns, E. (1997) *The Corner—A Year in the Life of an Inner-City Neighborhood*, New York, NY: Broadway Books.

Sinha, J. (2001) *The History and Development of the Leading International Drug Control Conventions*, Ottawa, Ontario: Parliamentary Research Branch, Library of Parliament.

Sloman, L. (1979) *Reefer Madness—Marijuana in America*, New York, NY: Grove.

Smith, K. and Flatley, J. (2011) *Drug Misuse Declared: Findings from the 2010/11 British Crime Survey England and Wales*, Home Office Statistical Bulletin, London: Home Office Statistics.

Smith, M.A. (1988) "The drug problem—is there an answer?," *Federal Probation* 52: 3–6.

Smith, M.E., Sviridoff, M., Sadd, S., Curtis, R. and Grinc, R. (1992) *The Neighborhood Effects of Street-Level Drug Enforcement—Tactical Narcotics Teams in New York—An Evaluation of TNT*, New York, NY: Vera Institute.

Sommers, I. and Baskin, D. (2006) "Methamphetamine use and violence," *Journal of Drug Issues* 36: 77–96.

——(2004) *The Social Consequences of Methamphetamine Use*, New York, NY: Edwin Mellen Press.

Sommers, I., Baskin, D. and Baskin-Sommers, A. (2006) "Methamphetamine use among young adults: health and social consequences," *Addictive Behaviors* 31: 1469–76.

Spector, M. and Kitsuse, J.I. (1987) *Constructing Social Problems*, New York, NY: Aldine de Gruyter.

Sterling, E.E. (2004) "Drug policy: a challenge of values," *Journal of Religion and Spirituality in Social Work* 23: 51–81.

Stolz, B.A. (2005) "Educating policymakers and setting the criminal justice policymaking agenda: interest groups and the 'Victims of Trafficking and Violence Act of 2000'," *Criminal Justice* 5: 407–30.

——(2002) "The roles of interest groups in US criminal justice policy making: who, when, and how," *Criminal Justice* 2: 51–69.

Substance Abuse and Mental Health Services Administration (SAMHSA) (2012) *The DAWN Report: Highlights of the 2010 Drug Abuse Warning Network (DAWN) Findings on Drug-Related Emergency Department Visits*, Rockville, MD: SAMHSA Center for Behavioral Health Statistics and Quality.

——(2011) *Results from the 2010 National Survey on Drug Use and Health: Summary of National Findings*, NSDUH Series H-41, HHS Publication No. (SMA) 11-4658, Rockville, MD: Substance Abuse and Mental Health Services Administration, http://www.samhsa.gov/data/NSDUH/2k10Results/Web/HTML/2k10Results.htm#Ch7 (accessed July 2, 2012).

Sutherland, E.H. and Cressey, D.R. (1974) *Criminology* (9th edn), Philadelphia, PA: J.B. Lippincott Company. (Originally published as *Criminology* by E.H. Sutherland, 1924.)

Sykes, G. and Matza, D. (1957) "Techniques of neutralization: a theory of delinquency," *American Journal of Sociology* 22: 664–70.

Szasz, T. (1982) "The psychiatric will—a new mechanism for protecting persons against 'psychosis' and psychiatry," *The American Psychologist* 37: 762–70.

Taylor, B.G., Brownstein, H.H., Mulcahy, T.M., Hafford, C., Woods, D. and Fernandes-Huessy, J. (2011a) "The characteristics of methamphetamine markets and their impact on communities," *Criminal Justice Review* 36: 312–31.

Taylor, B.G., Brownstein, H.H., Mulcahy, T.M., Woods, D., Fernandes-Huessy, J. and Hafford, C. (2011b) "Illicit retail methamphetamine markets and related local problems: a police perspective," *Journal of Drug Issues* 41: 327–58.

Taylor, I.R., Walton, P. and Young, J. (1973) *The New Criminology: For a Social Theory of Deviance*, London and New York, NY: Routledge & Kegan Paul.

Trebach, A.S. (1986) "The loyal opposition to the war on drugs—drugs and criminal law in Western democracies," paper delivered at the Conference on the Occasion of the Centenary of the Dutch Criminal Code, Amsterdam, September 4.

——(1982) *The Heroin Solution*, New Haven, CT: Yale University Press.

Trebach, A.S. and Zeese, K.B. (eds) (1990) *The Great Issues of Drug Policy*, Washington, DC: The Drug Policy Foundation.

Trostle, J., Bronfman, M. and Langer, A. (1999) "How do researchers influence decision-makers? Case studies of Mexican policies," *Health Policy and Planning* 14: 103–14.

UK Drug Policy Commission (2009) *Refocusing Drug-Related Law Enforcement to Address Harms—Full Review Report*, London: UK Drug Policy Commission, http://www.ukdpc.org.uk/reports.shtml (accessed July 4, 2012).

United Nations (UN) (1988) *United Nations Conference for the Adoption of a Convention Against Illicit Traffic in Narcotic Drugs and Psychotropic Substances*, http://www.unodc.org/pdf/convention_1988_en.pdf (accessed June 5, 2012).

——(1971) *The Convention on Psychotropic Substances, 1971*, http://www.unodc.org/pdf/convention_1971_en.pdf (accessed June 5, 2012).

——(1961) *Single Convention on Narcotic Drugs, 1961*, http://www.unodc.org/pdf/convention_1961_en.pdf (accessed June 5, 2012).

United Nations Information Service (UNIS) (2005) "Critical shortage of drugs for pain relief, says INCB," http://www.unis.unvienna.org/unis/pressrels/2005/unisnar899.html (accessed May 15, 2012).

United Nations Office on Drugs and Crime (UNODC) (2011) *World Drug Report 2011*, Vienna: United Nations.

——(2007) *World Drug Report 2007*, Vienna: United Nations.

van Laar, M., Cruts, G., van Gageldonk, A., van Ooyen-Houben, M., Croes, E., Meijer, R. and Ketelaars, T. (2011) *Report to the EMCDDA by the Reitox National Focal Point*, final version as approved by the Scientific Committee of the Netherlands National Drug Monitor (NDM), December 22, 2010, European Monitoring Centre for Drugs and Drug Addiction.

Van Niekerk, J.P. de V. (2011) "Time to decriminalise drugs?," *South African Medical Journal* 101: 79–80.

Walker, S. (2011) *Sense and Nonsense about Crime, Drugs, and Communities* (7th edn), Belmont, CA: Wadsworth.

Washington University Law Review (2010) "Shake and bake: the meth threat and the need to rethink 21 U.S.C. § 841 (C)(2)," 88 Wash. U.L. Rev.: 993–1020, 2010–11.

Weber, M. (1947) *The Theory of Social and Economic Organization* (translated by A.M. Henderson and T. Parsons and edited with an Introduction by T. Parsons), New York, NY: Free Press.

Weil, A. (1972) *The Natural Mind—An Investigation of Drugs and Higher Consciousness*, Boston, MA: Houghton Mifflin.

Weisheit, R.A. (1990) "Civil war on drugs," in R.A. Weisheit (ed.), *Drugs, Crime and the Criminal Justice System*, Cincinnati, OH: Anderson, pp. 1–10.

Weisheit, R. and White, W.L. (2009) *Methamphetamine: Its History, Pharmacology, and Treatment*, Center City, MN: Hazelden.

Welch, M., Wolff, R. and Bryan, N. (1998) "Decontextualizing the war on drugs: a content analysis of NIJ publications and their neglect of race and class," *Justice Quarterly* 15: 719–42.

Wheeldon, J. and Heidt, J. (2007) "Bridging the gap: a pragmatic approach to understanding critical criminologies and policy influence," *Critical Criminology* 15: 313–25.

Williams, T. (1992) *Crackhouse—Notes from the End of the Line*, New York, NY: Penguin Books.

Wilson, J.Q. and Herrnstein, R.J. (1985) *Crime and Human Nature*, New York, NY: Simon and Schuster.

Wisotsky, S. (1986) *Breaking the Impasse in the War on Drugs*, New York, NY: Greenwood.

Witkin, G. (1991) "The men who created crack," *U.S. News and World Report* August: 44–53.

Woolgar, S. and Pawluch, D. (1985) "Ontological gerrymandering: the anatomy of social problems explanations," *Social Problems* 33: 159–62.

World Health Organization (WHO) (2007) *Access to Controlled Medications Programme*, WHO/PSM/OSM/2007 2, Geneva: WHO.

——(2001) *Legal Status of Traditional Medicine and Complementary/Alternative Medicine: A Worldwide Review*, Geneva: WHO.

——(2000) *Narcotic and Psychotropic Drugs: Achieving Balance in National Opioids Control Policy. Guidelines for Assessment*, Geneva: WHO.

Young, J. (1987) "The tasks facing a realist criminology," *Contemporary Crises* 11: 337–56.

Zahn, M.A., Brownstein, H.H. and Jackson, S.L. (eds) (2004) *Violence—From Theory to Research*, Newark, NJ: LexisNexis.

Zimmer, L. (1987) "Operation pressure point: the disruption of street-level drug trade on New York's Lower East Side," *Occasional Papers from the Center for Research in Crime and Justice*, New York, NY: New York University School of Law.

Zinberg, N.E. (1984) *Drug, Set, and Setting: The Basis for Controlled Intoxicant Use*, New Haven, CT: Yale University Press.

INDEX

addiction 88
Afghanistan 4, 5
Akers, R.L. 47
alcohol 87
allopathic medicine 48–9
ammonium nitrate 81
analgesics 2–5
Analysis of S. 1918 21–2
anhydrous ammonia 81
anomie 29–30
Anslinger, H.J. 7, 52–6, 73
Anti-Drug Abuse Act 1988 7, 73
aspirin 88
assumptions 9, 12, 13, 27, 28, 63, 67, 89
Attaran, A. 96
attitudes 10

Baan Commission 38–9
background assumptions 12
Bahamas, the 61
Baltimore 76–7
Bayer Company 6
Beccaria, C. 46
Beck, A.J. 24–5
beliefs 10, 52–6, 90
Bennett, W. 7, 25, 26, 73
Best, J. 16, 35
Bible 62

biological positivism 30, 64–5
black Americans 66; *see also* race
Blumer, H. 9
Blumstein, A. 24–5
Booker, C. 31–2
Bronx, the 20
Burns, E. 76–7
Bush, G.H.W. 7, 25, 73

caffeine 87
Canada 83
cannabis *see* marijuana
Central and Eastern Europe 48
Christie, C. 95
Christie, N. 33
claims-making marketplace 15–16, 35
Clarke, R.V. 46
class 11, 34, 59–60, 90–1
cleaning products 82
Coca-Cola 6
cocaine 6, 11, 71, 87, 88; crack *see* crack cocaine
cold medicines 78, 80, 82
Combat Methamphetamine Epidemic Act 2005 78, 79
Common Sense for Drug Policy 17
communication technologies 92–4
communities of interest 93

control and regulation 11, 18, 20–36, 69, 90, 91, 95; alternative directions and questions to consider 31–6; social, cultural, and historical context 23–6; theoretical foundations 26–31
Convention against Illicit Traffic in Narcotic Drugs and Psychotropic Substances 8, 26
Convention on Psychotropic Substances 8, 26
Cooper, C.R. 53
Cornish, D.B. 46
crack cocaine 11, 71–7, 91
Cressey, D.R. 13–14, 15, 96–7
crime: link between marijuana and 52–6; violent *see* violence; war on 14, 97
Criminal Justice Policy Foundation 17
criminological theory 11–14; *see also* critical criminological theory, mainstream criminological theory
critical criminological theory 12–13, 90–1, 94; control and regulation 32–5; harm reduction 49–50; values 67–9
crystal meth 79, 82
cultural context: control and regulation 23–6; harm reduction 40–3; values 56–61
cultural criminological theory 68
Cuomo, M. 21
Currie, E. 14–15, 35, 90–1, 94, 97
Czech Republic 48

definition of drugs 86–9
DeKeseredy, W.S. 50
demand side efforts 27
demonization 6, 7
Des Jarlais, D. 42–3, 45
devaluation of drugs and drug users 57, 61–3
developing countries 3–4, 84–5
dextroamphetamine 88
differential association 46–7

discourse: informing 15–17; need for open and honest 96–7; public discourse 91–4, 94–5
discretion 38
Drug Enforcement Administration (DEA) 7, 86–7
Drug Policy Alliance 17
Duster, T. 11, 57

Eastern and Central Europe 48
ecstasy 87
Enlightenment 46
European Monitoring Centre for Drugs and Drug Addiction 39
evidence-based policy 48
explanations 89

Facebook 93
Federal Bureau of Narcotics (FBN) 7
Federal Drug Administration (FDA) 86
felony drug arrests 24
Freestyle Foundation, The 17
Fuhrman, E.R. 12

Galiber, J. 20–2, 23
gender 11, 34, 91
Ghodse, H. 3
Global Commission on Drug Policy 48, 96
Goldstein, A. 64–5, 88
Gottfredson, M. 29
Gouldner, A. 12

Hamilton, M.B. 9–10
harm reduction 7–8, 18, 37–51, 69, 90, 91, 95; alternative directions and questions to consider 48–51; social, cultural, and historical context 40–3; theoretical foundations 43–7
Harm Reduction International 40
Harm Reduction Journal 40
Harrison Act 1914 6–7
Hatty, S. 34
healthcare 48–9

Healy, M. 60
heroin 4–5, 55, 88
Heroin 6
Hirschi, T. 29
historical context: control and regulation 23–6; harm reduction 40–3; history of drug policy 5–8; values 56–61
home remedies 5–6
homicide 74
Hulsman Commission 38–9
Huxley, A. 1

ideologues 16, 92
ideology 9–15, 16, 27–8, 63, 89–90
ill-informed policy 82–5
import markets, methamphetamine 79, 81–2
imprisonment 23–5
Inciardi, J. 57
India 48–9, 61
Ingram, H. 27
international cooperation 8, 26
International Day Against Drug Abuse and Illicit Trafficking 61
International Narcotics Control Board (INCB) 3
International Opium Commission 8
International Society for the Study of Drug Policy 17
internet 92–3

Kaplan, J. 56
Kerala, India 61
King, M.L. 66
Kuhn, T.S. 10–11

labeling theory 65–6, 68
Lance Armstrong Foundation 62
Law Enforcement Assistance Administration (LEAA) 14
learning theory 47
left realism 50, 68–9
legalization 22
Leshner, A. 10
Literary Digest, The 40

LIVESTRONG.COM 62
local meth cooks 80–1
local mom-and-pop labs 79–80
local sales representatives 82
Lombroso, C. 30, 64
Los Angeles Times 60
LSD 87

McBride, D. 79
MacCoun, R. 38, 39
McKetin, R. 84
mainstream criminological theory 12–13, 90, 95, 97; control and regulation 29–31, 32; harm reduction 45–7; values 64–6
management *see* harm reduction
marijuana 7, 11, 87, 88; Anslinger 52–6; drug policy in the Netherlands 37–9
Marijuana Tax Act 1937 6–7, 55–6
marketplace of claims 15–16, 35
markets: crack cocaine 72–3, 74–7; methamphetamine 72–3, 77–82
Marlatt, G.A. 44
Mather, L. 2–3
media 57–60, 92–4
medicine, allopathic and traditional 48–9
methadone maintenance programs 41
methamphetamine 72–3, 77–84; markets 72–3, 77–82
Mexican drug cartels 79, 81–2
Mexico 83
mom-and-pop labs 79–80
morphine 2–5, 6, 84–5
Musto, D. 6, 57

Nadelmann, E. 94–5
naproxen 88
Narcotics Penalties and Enforcement Act 75
National Drug Control Strategy reports 25, 26–7, 73–4

National Drug Strategy Network 17
National Institute on Drug Abuse (NIDA) 86
National Institutes of Health (NIH) 10
National Survey on Drug Use and Health (NSDUH) 41–2
needle exchange programs 41, 42–3
Netherlands, the 7–8, 37–9
New York City 20, 59, 72, 74–6
New York Post 59–60
New York State 20–2, 23–4
New York Times 95
news media 92–3
Nickerson, J.W. 96
nicotine 87
Nixon, R. 7, 25, 73
norms, social 29–30

Obama, B. 26–7
Office of National Drug Control Policy (ONDCP) 7, 17, 25, 26–7, 73, 86
Oman 61
one-pot meth production 80–1
OpenBible.info 62
opioid analgesics 2–5
opium poppy cultivation 4–5
oxycodone 88

pain relief 2–5
participatory justice 33
peacemaking criminology 32–4
Pepinsky, H. 32–3
policing, saturation model of 75–7
policy-making process 16, 91–2
positive functions of drugs 1–2, 28–9, 48–50, 87–8
postmodern criminological theory 34
poststructural criminological theory 34
postulations 12
poverty 90–1
powder cocaine 71

precursor chemicals 77–8, 79, 80, 82, 84
prohibition 7, 11, 26
pseudoephedrine 77–8, 80, 81, 84
public discourse 91–4, 94–5
public health approach 40–3; *see also* harm reduction
punishment 46; imprisonment 23–5
Pure Food and Drug Act 1906 6

race 11, 34, 59–60, 91
Raspberry, W. 66
rational choice theory 46
Reagan, R. 7, 25
reality 15–16
recreational use 87
Reddit 31–2, 93
Reefer Madness 57–8
regulation and control *see* control and regulation
research grants 10
Reuter, P. 38, 39
Rockefeller, N. 23
Rockefeller's Drug Law 23
root causes 15, 94, 97
Ross, E. 29
Rutte, M. 39

saturation policing model 75–7
Schutz, A. 34
Schneider, A. 27
Schwartz, M. 34, 68
science 9–15, 16, 89–90
Science Museum, London 87
segregation 57
self-control 29
Senate Bill 1918 20–2, 23
shake-and-bake meth production 80–1
Simon, D. 76–7
Single Convention on Narcotic Drugs 8, 26
Sinha, J. 8, 26
smurfing 80
social class 11, 34, 59–60, 90–1

social constructionist theorists 15–16, 35
social context: control and regulation 23–6; harm reduction 40–3; values 56–61
social control 29; *see also* control and regulation
social disorganization theorists 30
social learning theory 47
social networking media 93
social norms 29–30
social order 28–9
social scientists 16, 92
South African Medical Journal 95
South America 95
Stars and Stripes United 17
Sterling, E. 56–7
stigmatization 66
Substance Abuse and Mental Health Services Administration (SAMHSA) 41–2
super labs 81–2
supply side efforts 27
Sutherland, E. 46–7
syringe exchange programs (SEPs) 41, 42–3
Szasz, T. 9

Tactical Narcotics Team (TNT) program 75–6
theorists 92
theory 9–15, 89–90; *see also* criminological theory, critical criminological theory, mainstream criminological theory
therapeutic use of drugs 48–9, 87–8; morphine and pain relief 2–5
tourism 37
traditional medicine 48–9
trafficking of drugs 5, 7; methamphetamine 79, 81–2
Treasury Department 54
treatment for drug abuse 26, 41–2
Twitter 93

understanding the drug problem 94–5
unintended consequences 72–3, 76, 80–5
United Kingdom (UK) 8, 40, 44
United Kingdom Drug Policy Commission 44
United Kingdom Harm Reduction Alliance (UKHRA) 43–4
United Nations: International Day Against Drug Abuse and Illicit Trafficking 61; three conventions 8, 26
United Nations Conference for the Adoption of a Convention Against Illicit Traffic in Narcotic Drugs and Psychotropic Substances 84
United Nations Office on Drugs and Crime (UNODC) 4, 5, 83, 84
United States drug policy 96–7; control and regulation 20–2, 23–5, 26–7, 35; crack cocaine case study 71–7; evolution over time 11; harm reduction 40, 41–3; history 5–7; methamphetamine case study 72–3, 77–84; unintended consequences for other countries 83; values 52–60; war on drugs *see* war on drugs
Uruguay 95
uses of drugs 28–9, 87–8

values 18, 52–70, 89–90, 91; alternative directions and questions to consider 66–70; guiding drug policy 9–15, 16; social, cultural, and historical context 56–61; theoretical foundation 61–6
van Laar, M. 39
violence: link with marijuana 52–6; related to crack cocaine 74, 76–7; related to methamphetamine 79

war on crime 14, 97
war on drugs 7, 11, 25, 57, 73, 94–5; Booker's critique of 31–2; Currie's critique of 14–15, 35, 90–1, 94; failure of 95–6
Weber, M. 34

websites 92–3
Weil, A. 2
World Drug Report 83
World Health Organization (WHO) 3–4

Yahoo! Answers 58–9